PULL YOURSELF
TOGETHER

PULL YOURSELF TOGETHER

OWNING YOUR DIFFERENCE
TO GET AHEAD

KATE JOHNSON

NEW DEGREE PRESS

PULL YOURSELF TOGETHER

Owning Your Difference to Get Ahead

ISBN   978-1-64137-262-6 *Paperback*

978-1-64137-263-3 *Ebook*

To Amber, my Co-Pilot

CONTENTS

"Your own Self-Realization is the greatest service you can render the world."

—RAMANA MAHARSHI

INTRODUCTION

"I was raised by a wonderful mother in the rough and tumble public housing projects on the Lower East Side of Manhattan," says Ursula Burns.

"Many people told me I had three strikes against me. I was black. I was a girl. And I was poor."

"Mom didn't see it that way. She constantly reminded me that where I was didn't define who I was. She knew education was my way up and out. On a modest salary, Mom somehow managed to send me to good Catholic schools. Back then I was prepared for one of three career options: nun, teacher, or nurse."

"None of those paths felt quite right for me and I began to dream of becoming an engineer. Brooklyn Polytechnic Institute offered me a spot in the freshman class and I panicked—a classic case of being careful what you wish for. I didn't have the right preparation. The school was in a different borough of New York City that seemed foreign and distant. I feared the students would surely be smarter than me."[1]

Burns was named president of Xerox Corporation in 2007 and chief executive officer in 2009, becoming the first African-American woman to lead a Fortune 500 company. In her first five years as CEO, she transformed Xerox into a thriving international services provider and made it profitable.

She was different.

And that *was* her greatest advantage.

Being different is *your* competitive advantage.

* * *

I grew up as a boundless person trapped in a normal person's body. My parents used to argue over who had the privilege

---

1   (Burns, 2019)

of waking me up in the morning because I would spring out of bed like it was Christmas—on an average day.

Sometimes it was too much.

At least that was a message I heard growing up. That my difference was too much. It wasn't just the decibels or the energy. It was the closeted queerness. It was my penchant for unbridled optimism in the midst of disaster. And for doing the things the opposite way of how other people were doing them.

I am a lesbian born in North Carolina who had no idea how to launch or navigate her career with all that *female-gay-bigness*. I faced discrimination, prejudice, and tragedies at a young age. It was all compounded by my mother dying from cancer when I was nineteen.

When I was finishing my undergraduate degree at UNC Chapel-Hill in 2007, I yearned for tailored advice from someone who understood. I needed to hear and know, "Companies need *you*, Kate." Instead I heard the generic, pat on the head advice:

Kate, you have a great degree, skills, and work experience, so get out there!

But how could I muster the bravery to get out there knowing how much baggage I carried? How could I trust my new environments? How would I know they would accept me? What should I do with myself?

I knew at a basic level I could get jobs. Yet I wasn't confident I could one day have influence and power as an Other. I saw my peers, cultural norms, and people who were in leadership roles and assumed I needed to conform. Like many misguided young people, I thought:

Don't I need to be more like everybody else to have a future with a major employer?

The answer may surprise you.

* * *

The United States has a well-known and storied history of segregation and discrimination in the workplace. For a long time, it was common knowledge that to get ahead meant you needed to be white, male, or exude traits of whiteness and maleness.

Fortunately for the betterment of all of us, those environments and thinking have evolved. This has happened in two ways: 1) changes in US employment and labor laws regarding discriminatory practices and 2) workplace Diversity & Inclusion (D&I) initiatives originating in influential companies and spreading to organizations of all shapes and sizes.[2]

I was deeply inspired to learn about workplace Diversity & Inclusion—and have benefited greatly from it in real life—so much so that I set out to write a book on it. But what I found in the process of researching this milieu was sobering.

The story goes like this: while organizations have made considerable progress in terms of protections for minorities and overall representation, they have made limited progress in getting minorities *into positions of power at scale.* You might see a handful of women on the company executive board. Maybe there are some people of color in line jobs (positions with profit and loss responsibility) or a noticeable manager who is out of the closet. But you will hardly see—even in 2019—an influential organization with a fully diverse board, C-suite, middle management, or overall composition in the numbers that mirror the US population.

Honestly, Diversity & Inclusion practitioners are *frustrated.* The work is hard, takes time, and just because you have all the right levers in place doesn't mean that minorities trust their employers. There's a lot of burnout and resentment in

---

2   (McCormick, 2007)

the profession and it was hard in my research to find answers. I talked to seasoned, influential D&I change agents at major organizations, and the main answer to "So what do the rest of us do?" was:

Be more inclusive.

Crickets.

This messaging is a problem. The broad D&I narrative has become focused on the betterment of society and righting wrongs and has become completely useless to those of us who are different and looking to shape influential careers. Yes, I should be more inclusive (as you should be too).

But then what?

What emerged in my research was an amazing series of stories around successful and high-performing, diverse players in the workplace game. These people have found paths *around or through* the prejudice and discrimination, leveraging their experience as an Other.

Let's move on from platitudes like "we should all be more inclusive" to a world where those of us who have been excluded from the power game dive deep on mastering its moves.

It's time for individual, diverse careerists to win the game and get ahead.

It's time to change the narrative. Our narrative.

* * *

This book is about how you can confidently do the work to gain access and bring value to organizations—to become a top performer as the person you were born to be. An army of change agents is working to make those organizations better in the long run for us.

We're going to explore how to move beyond the uncertain and common career advice of "bringing your whole self to work" to true action. This is about cultivating and developing individual power and distinction while reversing the view that the unique parts of yourself hold you back.

Companies need workers who are different. They need talent who deeply understand their diverse customers and help them connect with new and different markets. The broader marketplace is moving at such tremendous speed—and not to mention the mind-boggling technological revolutions of today—that companies can no longer afford to discriminate or staff themselves in a homogeneous way.

People are messy. Workplaces are messy. The trick is diverse high performers have found a way to organize the parts of themselves to excel in a prescribed professional setting while preserving and cultivating their uniqueness enough to stand out.

They have found a way to pull themselves together. They know themselves intimately and use their differences to have a competitive advantage—by bringing unusual backgrounds, perspectives, ideas, and skills to companies in desperate need of growth and innovation.

Here's how we're going to pull you together to give you a competitive advantage:

The Four E's

- **Explore.** Find the personal and professional spaces you want to occupy.
- **Energize.** Generate the support, energy, inspiration, and drive to overcome opposition and prejudice.
- **Engage.** Opportunities always come. Prepare for them and leverage your toolkit when they arrive.
- **Expand.** Get in the game and test your limits!

* * *

This book is for those who feel like the "Other" in the room. This is for women, people of color, LGBTQIA, and everyone in between.

In this book you'll see how:

- **Carla Harris** became the Managing Partner of Morgan Stanley by being negatively motivated.
- **Arlan Hamilton** used her access to queer, black, and female networks to become a novel venture capitalist.
- **Tess Holliday** took the brutal fashion world by storm as the first plus size-twenty-two model to be signed with a top agency and land the covers of *Cosmopolitan* and *People*.
- **Jacob Tobia** found coming out as an artist to be as difficult and as powerful as owning themselves as gender-queer.
- **Fiona Grant** was promoted into senior roles at Accenture *because* she was out of the closet.
- **Ellen Pao** paved the way for women to have greater power and influence in the harshest of male-dominated environments: Venture Capital.

And more!

* * *

Ursula Burns originally joined Xerox in 1980 as an engineer. She worked in a healthy progression of roles throughout the 1980s until a day in 1989 that would change everything.

During a company meeting, an employee asked Executive Vice President Wayland Hicks why Xerox was "so focused on diversity."

Ursula describes the event, "He didn't say 'black people,' he said, 'Why are we hiring all these different types of people and women?'"

She wasn't sold on the explanation given by Hicks and stood up in front of the meeting and "chided him for displaying a lack of passion and principles." The two shared an "unfriendly exchange."

"I thought I was going to be fired," says Ursula.[3]

Instead, though Hicks reproached Ursula for her tone, the two continued their discussion over several meetings. And just a year later he offered Ursula an executive assistant role that introduced her to the C-suite and changed the course of her career. The move gave her a front row seat to how executives ran a global business.

---

3   (Alesci, 2017)

She describes that assistant job as "the most important she's ever held."[4]

* * *

You don't need to be like everyone else to shape a powerful career. In fact, leveraging your difference can be an even greater source of power.

If you know how to do it.

It took me ten years to evolve into a confident, minority careerist. This book reveals the strategy of self-discovery I used to make the incredible leap from nonprofit work to landing a job at one of the most influential organizations in the world—McKinsey & Company.

In my time with both McKinsey & Company and Duke University, I have interviewed and counseled successful people from diverse and non-diverse backgrounds alike.

I wrote this book to show you how to get ahead. Being you.

It is time to Pull Yourself Together.

---

4   (Elk, 2017)

PART 1

EXPLORE

[investigate; search; test; try; delve into]

The process starts with the freedom to try; to experiment. You need to look around at different environments and ask yourself where you want to be. 'Should's are not the point. Follow your compulsions. Give yourself time and many chances.

This Part is about self-permission. Even if you don't see anyone like you in a space, you're allowed to want to be there.

CHAPTER 1

GETTING PAST BARISTA

"Always remember that you are absolutely unique. Just like everyone else."

—MARGARET MEAD

AN INTERNSHIP LAUNCHES A THOUSAND QUESTIONS

I had one summer internship in college.

It was 2006—the summer before my senior year—and I was obsessed with service and giving back to the community. At a career fair, I had stumbled upon a nonprofit called National Student Partnerships (now called Lift). Founded by college students, Lift staffed resource centers with student volunteers to help low-income residents find housing, jobs, gain access to government services, tax preparation, and any other resources possible.

A huge tenet of the work was helping our clients draft résumés. A résumé is a powerful document in that setting—a tangible output, quick to produce, and it eliminated many barriers to finding a job.

Just because our clients didn't have a résumé didn't mean they lacked skills. Most had a variety of jobs and even full-on careers yet hit setbacks and unexpected challenges, which made employment difficult.

As much as I was eager to help, and despite thorough training from Lift, it was intimidating to instruct someone else on a résumé. Every day I came to the office with the same doubt:

I am twenty-one years old and have never worked full time. Who am I to coach someone on his or her career?

As with most college kids, I had set out that summer hoping to gain insights into what I wanted to do with my own career. The clock was ticking and I needed to know where I was going. It was hard to reconcile the basic need for my first job and simultaneous yearning for a calling. Service and nonprofit work seemed a natural solution.

I relished that summer with Lift—meeting scrappy, resilient people and helping a noticeable group of clients. Many found new jobs, housing, and access to resources they couldn't achieve before working with us.

I wish this story ended with "and then it all made sense and I graduated college and found my dream job." Instead, I finished the summer with more questions about careers and jobs than when I started. I had found purpose in helping others and cultivated some tangible skills, but I'd found no way to healthily separate (or incorporate) my identity into what I would be doing as a profession. It all boiled down to:

How does who I am play into what I am going to do? And how can who I am be an asset?

These are classic questions. And also ones most people either skip over or rush too quickly to answer. It took me ten years to become the integrated and effective professional I dreamed of being back in that summer of 2006.

Now I know there is a process high performers use to get there—one I want to share with you.

I finished college in 2007 and landed a classic entry-level job with a small real estate company—not exactly my calling—yet a place to start.

* * *

evo·lu·tion

/e-və-ˈlü-shən/

noun

a: a process of change in a certain direction: UNFOLDING
b: the action or an instance of forming and giving something off: EMISSION
c (1): a process of continuous change from a lower, simpler, or worse to a higher, more complex, or better state: GROWTH
 (2): a process of gradual and relatively peaceful social, political, and economic advance
3: the process of working out or developing[5]

EVOLVING THROUGH THE FOUR E'S

We start out in this adult life as a mash-up of abilities, inherent traits, and experiences. We have a personality, we have tasks we've completed, and we have a set of life circumstances we've navigated. Somehow we're supposed to

---

5   Merriam-Webster, s.v. "evolution," accessed June 15, 2019, https://www.merriam-webster.com/dictionary/evolution.

translate that mash-up of our nature and nurture into something employable.

Highly successful people can take any tasks they've completed—whether paid or unpaid—and break them down into the skills they've utilized and cultivated. Every skill you have in this world counts.

What's more, they have found the effective ways to reveal and leverage enough of their unique personal qualities and background—in the execution of those skills—to stand out.

At its most basic level, this process is about self-discovery. Beyond the self-discovery, this process is about translating our intangible selves into something the market values above all others.

In business, if the market is asking for something rare, unique, or different and the "normal" sellers have nothing like that in their inventory, wouldn't you leap at the chance to fill that gap and reap the rewards? Similar to how sellers will test the market for a product, you can test out jobs, organizations, and your own labor markets for well, YOU.

Here's how to proceed:

1) **Explore.** Find the personal and professional spaces you want to occupy. This involves trial and error.

2) **Energize.** Generate the support, energy, inspiration, and drive to overcome opposition and prejudice. You're going to get pumped up!

3) **Engage.** Opportunities always come. Prepare for them and leverage your toolkit when they arrive. There is no room for sitting on the sidelines.

4) **Expand.** Get in the game and test your limits. At this point you are shamelessly influencing.

Let's go!

* * *

Adriane Armstrong
I remember that moment of being looked over.

"I grew up in Santa Barbara. It was in many ways like growing up on a movie set: very beautiful, palm tree-lined beaches, sparkly clean streets, gorgeous architecture; it was a very affluent town," describes Adriane Armstrong, CEO of non-profit social enterprise Juma Ventures.

"What a lot of people don't see is that it's a very segregated town. For me it was quite obvious because in almost every setting I was the only person of color (my mom is Filipino and my dad is white). I was the only student of color, and the only person of color in restaurants."

As early as elementary school [in the late 1980s], Adriane felt the effects of that segregation. "When I was seven years old in the second grade, I first saw how people were treated differently based on the color of their skin."

In the state of California, public school elementary students take a Gifted and Talented Education test (GATE) to determine tracking into rigorous academics as they age: specialized teaching, Honors courses, and eventually Advanced Placement (AP) classes in high school. This is a tracking system (also known as a streaming system) where students attend academic classes only with students whose overall academic achievement is the same as their own.[6]

"I was not even selected to take the test. My teachers looked over me and it took my parents going in to advocate for me to even take the test. I went on to have a successful academic career thereafter, but I remember that moment of being

---

6   *Wikipedia, The Free Encyclopedia*, s.v. "Gifted Education," (accessed June 15, 2019)

looked over," says Adriane, voice shaking as she describes the experience.

By the time Adriane entered high school in the mid-1990s, she noticed the results of that early testing, "I went to a beautiful public high school, again in an affluent town, and in many classes I was the only student of color. And the segregation was so striking that the AP and Honors classes for the kids that tracked into the GATE program were in the main hallway and the classes for those who did not test into the program, mostly Latino, were in the basement."

Undeterred, Adriane excelled in her studies and was accepted to Stanford University in 2000. The issues in her community inspired her to pursue a bachelor's in Comparative Studies and Race and Ethnicity in addition to a master's in Social Psychology and MBA with a focus in nonprofit management, all from Stanford.

In that time at Stanford, one moment brought her life's work to the forefront.

"I went to a talk from a professor visiting from UCLA on academic tracking, and her premise is that tracking really affects the outcomes of students based on the color of their skin. In some cases the overall test scores of a school can obfuscate the deep inequalities within the school. [She showed how] affluent schools with high test scores are where students of color will fare worse than they would at an inner city school. The examples she put up were of how students of color at Compton High would do better than students of color at Santa Barbara High—my own high school.

"In that moment I broke down in tears because it was a validation of everything I had experienced myself."

Aware of her own success, the experience at Stanford became the linchpin for her eventual leadership with Juma. "I was very privileged to be afforded those opportunities but I thought how easy it would have been for me to have been overlooked in that setting and situation."

When she was young and vulnerable, Adriane had allies (her parents and teachers) to ensure she wasn't looked over. As she aged, she took ownership of her future, becoming an advocate for youth and social justice and a leader driving social change.

* * *

JUMA VENTURES
Companies are not ready for the new consciousness of the next generation.

"We are experts at employing young people."

—ADRIANE ARMSTRONG

Founded in 1993 in San Francisco, Juma Ventures (friends simply call it Juma) is a nonprofit social enterprise that operates businesses with the purpose of employing young people. They make sure youth earn a paycheck, learn to manage their money and gain essential skills like responsibility, teamwork and how to communicate in the workplace.

"Ultimately, Juma connects youth to their next job and sets them on a path to a career."

Juma operates a social enterprise business, directly employing young people while supporting and guiding them with training and coaching. They also partner with large corporations to staff young people into entry-level jobs. What really sets Juma apart is their scale in both employing youth and providing social services, as they work with thousands of youth a year in six cities: Atlanta, Houston, Sacramento, San Francisco, San Jose, and Seattle.[7]

Juma focuses on the underserved, working with young people who have been disconnected from both school and work due to challenges and instability in their home lives. The youth need both education and work—to have a chance at careers—but cannot pursue them at the same time without support.

As Adriane Armstrong describes, "Addressing the barriers to work is a huge part of what we do: transportation, childcare, housing, etc. but we also coach them in mindsets. There's a lot to do around exposure, goal-setting, and growth mindset. We anchor on soft skills. If we specialize in anything, I would say it's sales and customer service, but we're not necessarily teaching them a technical skill.

"We think that's important because right now a lot of the jobs that require technical certifications and skills are being automated. So we teach them a growth mindset to be focused on learning, development, and education so they can stay ahead of the future of work," says Adriane.

---

7   (Juma Ventures, 2018)

"There's a huge opportunity in the job market. At any given time five million young people are disconnected from school and work, and there are five million open entry-level jobs. I'll also note that only 400,000 of those require coding skills; whereas, four million of them require soft skills. Again, I think soft skills are often overlooked.

"A lot of people in the Bay Area will ask me, 'Why aren't you getting youth into professional jobs? Why aren't you sending them to internships with tech companies?' The reality is that four out of five people who respond to me when I ask what their first job was will say 'food service' or 'newspaper delivery.'

"My own first job was as a barista. So the key question here is 'why could I go from barista to internship to career when some people are going to be baristas forever?'"

The answer to Adriane's question on why is that it cuts by race.

As Adriane describes, "What we're trying to unpack here [at Juma] is that, yes working in food service is great and is important work. But we need to address the systems that keep certain people in those jobs indefinitely while others get to go on to build careers."

SOFT SKILLS = YES

The common assumption is that your job success is all about your technical skills.

Wrong.

Only 15 percent of your job success comes from technical skills.

This is according to research released in 2016 by the Carnegie Foundation, Harvard University, and Stanford Research Center. The findings suggest 85 percent of job success comes from having well-developed soft or people skills.[8]

Soft skills are the way, and they're in high demand.

When assessment company Wonderlic surveyed employers in 2016, they found 93 percent of employers viewed soft skills as either an "essential" or a "very important" factor in hiring decisions.[9]

LinkedIn conducted its own surveys, and it found in 2015 that 59 percent of US hiring managers believe it's difficult to find candidates with soft skills.[10]

---

8   (Deming, 2015)
9   (Coursera, 2017)
10 (Berger, 2016)

Soft skills are hard to train and teach, and our current education system has struggled to address this in a scalable way. The more we can individually nurture and improve our soft skills the better.

* * *

Lauren Russo
I help people who are creative rebels.

Lauren Russo never planned to become a niche career coach—especially not an expert in advising creative professionals, many of whom are women of color.

Born in Florida, Lauren grew up in North Carolina and southwest Virginia. She had deep empathy for others and as she was later launching her career became fascinated with the question of, "How do people thrive?"

Attending the University of Virginia for her undergraduate studies, she spent time volunteering with women who had been victims of assault; she considered a path in counseling and advocacy, yet, "I feared the burnout I saw in others [who pursued the work]." Instead she chose roles in fundraising at UVA for a short time, which parlayed to working with *Iris Magazine*, the publication of the Women's Center. She started with the magazine in 2006 and eventually grew into an Associate Editor role.

The magazine featured a monthly story of a successful alumna, and the stories made an impression on Lauren.

"We would ask how did this person achieve success in their career? It was never A to Z, [rather] with a million stops in between. What was unspoken between me and my boss at the time, was to help young women in college let go of the devil of perfectionism."

Lauren and her peers at the magazine made sure to interview women from a breadth of backgrounds. "We also had the awareness that poor women, queer women, women of color, and disabled women are all facing a certain set of obstacles that traditional career success doesn't really account for...we liked to advocate for this idea that your life can look like whatever you want it to look like, whoever you are."

Over time the series sparked Lauren's inspiration—knowing she wanted to help people individually and work with them one on one—and after six years with the magazine, she realized her dream job was to be a life coach. "I would have strangers coming up and telling me their whole life stories without prompting; I was approachable... and I knew

I wanted to work with people in a way that was about building something."

She apprenticed in the Martha Beck Life Coaching Training Program with other coaches to become certified and narrow her coaching focus. "I was interested in how external structures affect us internally...whether that's broader culture or societal messages all the way to what our family and friends look like, even how our day is structured."

In 2012, she joined the Creative Executive coaching group in Austin and is still a full-time coach today.

The majority of Lauren's clients come to her through word of mouth. Her big break into consistent client work happened after one black female client saw tremendous results—and started referring her peers. Then Lauren realized her tools and interests could especially help people of color, in addition to a variety of "others," navigate a white, male-dominated working world.

"In terms of navigating the world of professionalism, our world works really well if you can work really hard and push it—if you have a lot of drive. Except having that kind of drive doesn't work for you if you are an identity type that rubs people the wrong way. Like if you're a woman or a black or brown person," says Lauren.

Underpinning the challenges minority groups face are organizational and societal structures which affect all workers.

"The working world is designed for people who can work really hard for a really long time, don't have any anxiety about it, are confident—even for those people… upper middle class white guys are eventually going to hit snags too.

"It's not actually built for workers. *It's built to get work out of people.* So if you have children, a disability, or an illness, these will pretty much stop you dead in your tracks."

"I help people who are creative rebels," says Lauren. "I work with people who don't fit the average mold based on race, gender, etc. but even more than that, based on personality— are highly creative." Many of her clients are at top creative agencies and influential retail and design companies.

As her niche has emerged, her passion for Diversity & Inclusion has become even stronger.

"When you're different you feel it. You have to psych yourself up to go out there," says Lauren.

Coaches like Lauren are here to psych you up and get you out there.

ACTION ITEMS FOR CAREER DOMINATION

MINDSET

Adopt a brand new mindset. I am no longer The Other. This is not about conformity. This is about getting honest with yourself about how you are not a victim or at a disadvantage by being different from the others in the room. Yes, you are different from them—and that's good.

We don't need more of Them. We need more You.

EXERCISE

Identify your inherent traits and personal experiences. Take a pen and paper and write out the intrinsic traits and life experiences that have influenced you most. These are the things you cannot change. Ask yourself, "Do I feel held back by any of these? If so, how can I make peace?"

Identify your skills. Make a list of all jobs, projects, tasks, and volunteer work—whether paid or unpaid. Write down the skills you gained or improved during each endeavor.

What is unique about you? Ask yourself this question not from the perspective of "How am I better than others?" but rather "What can I bring to the table that is rare, helpful, and valuable"?

CHAPTER 2

DIFFERENCE IS THE FUTURE OF WORK

———

"A pessimist sees the difficulty in every opportunity. An optimist sees the opportunity in every difficulty."

—WINSTON CHURCHILL

Distractions abound.

Are you listening to them?

Or are you listening to You?

LET'S STOP GIVING A SHIT ABOUT
THE FUTURE OF WORK

The future of work was one of the hottest trends in business in 2017 and 2018. People are obsessed with knowing what on earth we will be doing with ourselves and how will we make money at some unknown future date.

Naturally.

Will we be standing or sitting in our offices in some fascinating, magical arrangement optimized for hyper-productivity or miles apart with unfathomable technology while we work in our pajamas? Will the robots have taken over all of our jobs or just those of the people we don't like? Will we still be using annoying jargon and haggling over departmental budgets, or will future currencies explode our money discussions?

It's an exhausting conversation. Underneath it we're all worrying:

Will I have a job and can I make a living and a life?

Now, to organizations and institutions, the trends of future technology and work matter tremendously. As Anna Tunkel of *Forbes* writes:

Leading global institutions from the World Bank to MIT are launching new efforts and initiatives focused on understanding the evolution of jobs and addressing a key question—how can talent be developed and deployed to ensure that more than seven billion people can fulfill their potential?[11]

Seven billion people—the whole planet? How in the world can we shape our careers as individuals if we're struggling with the idea of how seven billion people work?

This is a distraction.

This is when the dialogue around the future of work becomes disempowering to those of us who have no control over any industry, market, supply/demand, or any other uncontrollable force around the workplace.

Let's be real. Let's bring our focus back to ourselves as individuals. We need to say:

I don't give a shit what the future of work is.

Let's get back to you—that one person. Your focus for your career needs to be on acquiring the skills and tools and

---

11   (Tunkel, 2018)

shaping yourself in ways that bring value to the workplace, *no matter what the future looks like.*

Luckily for you, you were born with a unique amalgam of qualities and have experiences no one else can replicate.

You have a style.

* * *

distinctive

dis·tinc·tive | \ di-ˈstiŋ(k)-tiv \

adjective

a: marking as separate or different: serving to distinguish
b: having or giving an uncommon and appealing quality: having or giving style[12]

Distinction is a more refined way of saying "standing out due to personal flair." There are a lot of ways to have flair. On a basic level, one needs to go above and beyond the task at hand. This can also include unique qualities or talents

---

12 Merriam-Webster, s.v. "distinctive," accessed June 15, 2019, https://www.merriam-webster.com/dictionary/distinctive.

(or background) or even utilizing skills atypical for the role you're in or compared to peers.

Let's look at Silicon Valley as an example.

According to Human Resources thought leader, and Deloitte Partner, Josh Bersin:

It turns out if you look at the data on the most in-demand skills in the San Francisco Bay area... which is the most in-demand job market in the United States... the number one skill [in 2018] that is the most in demand in San Francisco is oral communications. It's not machine learning. It's not software, it's not AI, it's not algorithms. It's communicating with people.[13]

Being distinctive—while seemingly challenging—can be pretty simple. You can actually stand out in Silicon Valley by being the technologist who knows how to talk about technology. Or by being the technologist who makes room at the table for people who are different.

* * *

---

13   (Bersin, 2016)

"Life's most persistent and urgent question is, 'What are you doing for others?'"

—MARTIN LUTHER KING, JR.

Morgan DeBaun
I wanted to create something that would be a reflection of who I was.

"I think I've always been entrepreneurial and tried to make things out of nothing and see how the world should be or how people should be treated and try to make that happen," says Morgan DeBaun, CEO of digital media platform Blavity and one of the most influential women in Silicon Valley.[14]

Morgan's entrepreneurial spirit started in middle school in the early 2000s. Back in the day there were no vending machines in her school, and rather than complaining (as most thirteen-year-olds would), she saw a possible business plan. "[It] then created this really great opportunity for me to go to Costco and buy up all the snacks and candy at a discount and sell it to people at school because they didn't have any machines."[15]

---

14   (Stahler, 2019)
15   (Stahler, 2019)

"When I was younger, I would look for opportunities to make money, invest, and create things. I didn't quite know where that would take me, but I knew I wanted to create something that would be a reflection of who I was. Blavity is a manifestation of just that," says Morgan.[16]

Morgan studied Entrepreneurship and Political Science at Washington University in St. Louis—a predominantly white institution. She became close friends with future Blavity cofounders Aaron Samuels, Jonathan Jackson, and Jeff Nelson. They regularly engaged in conversations over lunch so fulfilling and engaging—from politics to pop culture and beyond—that other black students were drawn to them.

"During our time at Washington University [the mid 2000s], there was a particular place where all of the Black students would sit together; and that was at the lunch table. Like in many groups and ethnicities in culture, food and gathering make people feel comfortable and at home despite the fact they may be amongst people they don't know. That lunch table is where the idea and the term 'Blavity' originated. We would sit down, then another person would sit down, and then another two or three people would sit down. Then, before we knew it, there would more than twenty of us sitting there for hours," says Morgan.[17]

16 (Mitchell, 2016)
17 (Mitchell, 2016)

"We would skip class and talk about critical race theories, what the Alphas did at the party, or whatever it may be. That moment when everyone would come to the table from different classes, parts of the country, and ethnicities of the diaspora—that was Black Gravity, or Blavity."[18] The group graduated in 2012 with strong job opportunities in consulting and tech, dabbling with the idea of a digital media connection on the side.

For Morgan, she accepted her first job after graduation with Intuit in 2012, growing as a product manager and engineer across 2.5 years.

A self-described, "tech girl," she spent her time with the company honing her chops on back-end work and learning how to lead. Without realizing the challenges many women were facing in tech, she fearlessly managed teams of male engineers unscathed.

As she describes, "Sometimes when you're in those moments, it's hard for you to absorb it because you can't afford to be distracted by how other people are treating you when it's negative."[19]

---

18   (Mitchell, 2016)
19   (Stahler, 2019)

She navigated by staying focused on what mattered to her, "I love innovation. I love technology, and I would never let male ego take away something I love. Right? It's a weird balance that I think a lot of women have to have."

In August of 2014, the shooting of Michael Brown in St. Louis gained national attention.

Morgan describes her reaction, "I felt completely helpless. I felt like I should be in St. Louis taking care of my city, but instead I'm sitting in a downtown San Francisco high-rise in a cubicle...And so at that moment it became apparent. There is a disconnect for me and also an information [disconnect] that the black community has in this country because we have not made it a priority to build our own new-age digital media brand that can distribute accurate information and stories that will never get covered anywhere else."

Her friends Aaron, Jonathan, and Jeff from WashU felt the same.

"They all felt like, 'Wow, I'm crushing it at my job. I'm loving the work that I do and I'm learning all the time, but I have this kind of emptiness in my personal life and in my... being because I just feel disconnected from my community because I've made this choice to be in a different type of field like Silicon Valley or Wall Street or becoming a doctor," says Morgan.

They decided to build a connection online, which emulated what they had in college—a full-fledged online forum for black millennials to discuss important issues.

* * *

BLACK + GRAVITY = BLAVITY

Morgan was only twenty-four years old when she and her co-founders launched Blavity, which now markets itself as, "one of the fastest growing digital media outlets on the web, reaching more than seven million millennials a month."[20]

Blavity has now branched out with sister sites Travel Noire, Shadow & Act, and a women's lifestyle site 21Ninety. The brand also hosts multiple yearly conferences such as Afro-Tech and Summit21—aimed at empowering and uplifting the black community.

Now twenty-eight, and with Blavity going strong—recently securing an additional $6.5 million in funding, one of the largest for a start-up run by a black woman—Morgan sees the diversity gaps in Silicon Valley clearly. "I think it's a shame. It doesn't make sense that in 2018, I am one of the highest black women in tech media."

---

20 (Blavity)

Maybe it does make sense.

UPSHOT

- **Your network can be powerful in many ways**: a source of support in troubling times, a channel for personal growth and development, and an obvious group of future customers.
- **Connecting with your network around meaningful ideas and values is the foundation of "networking."**

In 2018, Harvard Business School's Project on Managing the Future of Work and the Boston Consulting Group's Henderson Institute conducted a survey of 11,000 workers and 6,500 business leaders spanning eleven countries: Brazil, China, France, Germany, India, Indonesia, Japan, Spain, Sweden, the United Kingdom, and the United States. They focused on lower-income and middle-skills workers and surveyed them at companies different from the business leaders.

Their results were fascinating, "The two groups perceived the future in significantly different ways."

Predictably, business leaders feel anxious as they struggle to marshal and mobilize the workforce of tomorrow. In a climate of perpetual disruption, how can they find and hire employees who have the skills their companies need? And what should they do with people whose skills have become obsolete?

And the workers:

The workers, however, didn't share that sense of anxiety. Instead, they focused more on the opportunities and benefits the future holds for them, and they revealed themselves to be much more eager to embrace change and learn new skills than their employers gave them credit for.

One of the key findings of the study:

Workers are seeking more support and guidance to prepare themselves for future employment than management is providing.[21]

The survey underscores the damage of negative messaging from business leaders about our future is more about *their organizational* future.

Your distinctive future is bright.

* * *

---

21 (Fuller et al., 2019)

"I can't wring blood from a stone."

—SOHEIR KHASHOGGI

Christopher Lafayette
I saw that I had to build what I wanted to do.

"For the U.S. to compete on a global stage—whether it's emerging technologies that are happening, such as artificial intelligence, virtual reality, immersive technologies, or crypto-currencies— we have to make sure you [as a company] understand that you need to hire the people that you want to buy your products. If you don't, then you face failing in the global market," says Christopher Lafayette, Holodeck Builder and adviser to Technology companies, large and small.

Christopher works in the trenches of Diversity & Inclusion in Silicon Valley.

"I was born into D&I...I've started speaking more at conferences and broadly because it's gotten to a point where there just have to be more voices. I'm a technologist—which is where I'd rather be spending my time. But when you have so few African Americans who understand technology the way I do, you're almost obligated to become the speaker or voice for Diversity & Inclusion. Someone has to do it. I'm not alone.

Born and raised in California, Christopher was deeply enthusiastic for technology at a young age. He had a father passionate about computers, "My dad worked in IT at University of California at Berkeley. I was exposed early to it. But I ask myself, if I'm a young black man without a parent in the field, 'Where else am I going to find out about technology?' It's not impossible. But, when a kid sees their parents working in technology it has potential for remarkable influence."

When searching in Silicon Valley for work, Christopher targeted tech jobs and was surprised to find barriers from the get-go, "I saw that I had to build what I wanted to do."

Bootstrapping himself with an agency business and tech skills he honed through his own curiosity, Christopher started his first company in 2008—"an artisan media firm"—which led to a variety of organizations-- including a creative agency, online communities, and making Holodecks.

Over time, his small businesses landed influential clients in the Valley who started asking for his advice and connections to networks as a person of color, "Companies are committed to Diversity & Inclusion but are stalling when the return on investment (ROI) is not coming back from where they're investing it. We've got recruiters going to a myriad of career fairs and they're still not getting large numbers of diverse talent into companies. They're asking me, 'how do we make this work?'"

Many thought-leaders have dissected the plethora of reasons that Silicon Valley faces diversity challenges. Christopher boils it down to, "We keep observing tech companies where everyone in the decision-making rooms all come from Stanford, with no diversity of thought. It's one big homogeneous perspective."

For Christopher, "The last mile is about getting people jobs". He decided to advise organizations informally which grew into formal advising roles and initiatives.

"I've rallied a team to connect minority talent to companies, and worked specifically with non-profits who provide staffing. Companies have tapped me on the shoulder because they've not seen the ROI from the weekend camps and hack-a-thon's [they fund] that don't go far enough in making jobs happen."

Focusing on two major ways to influence, Christopher looks to 1) bridge networks and 2) train talent, "Recently a company came in from New York to a major tech conference I was attending and had no idea how to find diverse talent— they were not tapped into diverse networks there at all. We've [Chris' nonprofit partnerships] invested the time to connect pipelines from underrepresented communities to those companies. We've also invested in training to ensure that these companies are getting talent even more qualified than what they have now."

The work is arduous, bringing the interview barriers to light.

"We can't get them [underrepresented talent] to the interview process and then when we are, they're not making it through. We're concerned about what's being asked of them in the interview— we're seeing managers preferring to 'hire someone who is like me' from a white male perspective. The underrepresented talent also feels tremendous pressure during the interview to be what the companies want— it's emotionally challenging."

"Some companies will really listen to us and some won't when we tell them that their interview process—which they've had a long time— is not working for minority talent," says Christopher.

This emotional challenge reveals the nuances of different worlds and continues through offers and hires, "Once they're getting in the door— African Americans specifically— I think they're coming into a system not built on their culture. There's not a lot of parity and connection once the hire has been made. Internal operations and communications especially."

In Christopher's day job, he is immersed in topics rolled up into the larger Future of Technology conversation: artificial intelligence, virtual reality, tele-presence, and virtual media, "My perspective is coming from being a technology driver."

In 2018, he launched the Armada, described on its website:

"A Human Engine Machine"[22]

Christopher is obsessed with the ideas and intersections of technology and work, and yet spends a chunk of his time outside of his day-job on people issues— diverse people issues.

As Christopher says when you ask him about his mission, he'll respond, "I'm not asking for a hand-out from Silicon Valley. I'm extending a hand to help it".

UPSHOT

- **People like Christopher—at the intersections of business and diversity—are fighting hard for all of us.**
- **Being the personal bridge of diverse networks to Corporate America and other organizations is a powerful position.** Institutions need those bridges and are investing in them and taking action.

---

22 (Armada)

ACTION ITEMS FOR CAREER DOMINATION

MINDSET

My network will make or break me. Despite the negative rhetoric in the world or negative experiences we have all had, there is no greater truth or testament to mankind than how much we have helped one another. To set the stage for the power of "who you know," you must be clear on "the people I know matter." Open yourself up to the opportunities you can co-create with the people you know and values you share.

EXERCISE

Cultivate the habit of tracking and evaluating the strength of the relationships of your professional network. You can do this by hand, digitally, through an address book, Excel, contact manager, whatever works for you. Start here:

- Name
- Email, Phone, Social media connection or link
- Community you know them from: affinity network (cultural, gender identity, race, ethnic, etc.), former colleague, alumni group, utilized their professional services, met at conference, etc.
- Date of last interaction
- How you interacted (digital, phone, in person)

- What value you've brought to them over time: connected them with a person/service they needed, given advice, shared their content on your social sites, sent a thank you note, provided a reference, etc.
- Who haven't you helped/brought value to in your network?
- Peer level or more Senior?
- Big fish: those you haven't "been able to" help given their gravitas (you likely gained more value from the interaction than you thought you could offer them).

Grow your weak ties. Acquaintances are the people in your network who will practically help you the most at junctures where you are stuck. They are less biased and know less about you than your friends. Therefore, they can more efficiently get you to the right place when you're in transition. Practice asking weak ties—rather than your friends—for professional help when you need it.

CHAPTER 3

FROM SCAR TISSUE TO SUCCESS

———

"The two most important days in your life are the day you are born and the day you find out why."

—MARK TWAIN

You're at the beginning.

There will be pain.

It will take effort, sweat, and commitment.

You are not the favorite.

Are you still in?

DELIVERY

My wife told me before getting pregnant that she would give birth au naturel—vaginally and without medication. She made that declaration again in her first trimester, again in her second trimester, still again in her third trimester, and finally through gritted teeth during deep labor pains.

She was hella serious.

Let's talk about what this means. We live in a time where every medicine, comfort, doo-dad, and procedure to ease any and all birth pains is available to us at any local hospital. And my wife decided her beliefs about her child's health were different enough, and a larger priority, than making the birth "easier."

She was going to engage in the entire process without artificial relief or support.

Now if you know my wife, you wouldn't find any of this out of character. She's one of those people who chooses to do things *because* they are hard.

About ten years ago—as a very nonathletic adult—she wanted to enter triathlons. She investigated how to get started and saw the common first step that privileged suburban racers would take was to buy sleek, fifteen-pound carbon bikes at $3,000.

Her answer, "*Fuck that.*"

A friend had gifted her a twenty-five-pound steel, 1970s road bike (or shall we say "clunker") and she was happy to launch her training for free.

The satisfaction came for her eight months into her training at her first Olympic distance triathlon—when she was *passing* those guys on their fancy lightweight bikes. Not all of them, but most of them.

Noticeable was how miserable her competitors looked and their refusal to smile when they passed; whereas, my wife smiled *the whole damn race.* The fancy racers were obsessed with winning, having the best gear, and sweating the least.

She didn't care about any of that and enjoyed every morsel of every hard-fought mile.

My wife didn't win that race or subsequent races, but she proved her point. That she would find fulfillment through her own definition of achievement.

* * *

Labor

/ley-ber/

verb

1. to strive, as toward a goal; work hard
2. to act, behave, or function at a disadvantage
3. to be in the actual process of giving birth[23]

My wife spent over twenty hours deep in the hard labor to birth our little one. She sweated and rocked and groaned, mentally battled the waves of torrential pain and discomfort, heaved, and finally pushed out—for an ungodly period of moments and breaths—life.

This is exactly the process it takes to birth an extraordinary career.

---

23 Merriam-Webster, s.v. "labor," accessed June 15, 2019, https://www.merriam-webster.com/dictionary/labor.

If you want to distinguish yourself, you need to be ready to grind and reach and create.

You have to birth yourself.

* * *

Arlan Hamilton
There was a lot of stuff I had to prove.

"I grew up very quickly understanding that I was going to have to do more if I wanted to be seen as equal. I was going to have to work at least twice as hard if I was even going to be given a chance or taken seriously," says Arlan Hamilton.[24]

Arlan is the founder of Backstage Capital, a novel and acclaimed venture capital firm, which invests solely in minority entrepreneurs.

In 1995 and at age fifteen, Arlan found her first job at Pudge Brothers Pizza in Dallas, Texas. She began by taking phone orders and grew into other roles, "Soon I was doing the work of three people, essentially. It was the first time I understood that I'm going to do a lot of work for a lot less [money]."[25]

24 (Rodriguez, 2016)
25 (Stiffler, 2018)

Arlan parlayed a series of part-time jobs into the music business in the early 2000s. She worked as an usher at Cirque de Soleil, a security guard at a major music concert, and then manager for an indie Norwegian punk-pop band touring the US in a van.[26]

"I used to think I was so strange," Hamilton said. "None of my friends were taking risks like I was taking. They had jobs with health insurance."[27]

By 2012, Hamilton had risen in responsibilities and managed or produced major acts: Kirk Franklin, CeeLo Green, Amanda Palmer, and others. The hustle and skills she learned through her odd jobs translated well to wrangling bands, managing staff, and organizing tours.[28]

Around that time she noticed many of the artists and music executives in her circle were investing in tech start-ups—a world in which she wasn't familiar.

"I started becoming very curious about Silicon Valley and start-ups in general. While in Texas, I started remotely helping companies on small projects, and that turned

---

26 IBD
27 (Stiffler, 2018)
28 (Rodriguez, 2016)

into me remotely helping them connect with investors," says Hamilton.

"Over time, I started noticing a pattern. If I sent certain pitch decks that showcased companies with an all-white, male team, they would get to the next step, no matter what they were building. If the company had someone of color or a woman, there would be a push-back about not understanding the market, no matter what the market was."

This was striking to Arlan, who had strong networks as a queer woman of color in addition to her music and start-up networks.

"I started realizing that I was seeing a lot of companies very early, and I had a lot of trust with those founders, and we related well to each other. There was an opportunity there, and if I could put together some sort of pool, I could probably make money investing in companies that were overlooked."[29]

If she knew how to invest.

"To become a VC [venture capitalist], most people go through four years of school, or get an MBA. I thought, 'I can figure that out.' So I just did that at home.... I read every single blog

---

29   (Blodgett, 2017)

or book I could find. I watched hundreds of hours of video on YouTube."[30]

She read voraciously, going through books like *Venture Deals* by Brad Feld and Jason Mendelson. "They became sort of my professors at this four-year college that I created for myself," she says.[31]

Working with start-ups became a side project and passion.

Her first foray involved the idea of a fund focused on LGBT entrepreneurs, which she pursued for about six months in 2013. "I went hard on that, but it just didn't take off at all," she says. Hamilton had no credibility in the tech industry. "There was a lot of stuff I had to prove."[32]

Over time she also realized that she needed to be devoted to her investing path and step back from her music tour work. "Summer of 2014, I realized I would have to be all in because it was such an uphill battle. So, I stopped taking tour money for a short period of time. When I decided to focus, I got my first check from Susan Kimberlin, a former executive at Salesforce, and she is now our venture partner," says Hamilton.[33]

---

30 (CNBC,2018)
31 IBD
32 (Rodriguez, 2016)
33 (Blodgett, 2017)

Hamilton is describing meeting Susan Kimberlin at Y Combinator's Female Founders Conference in January of 2015 in San Francisco. The two gravitated to one another with similar theories that diversity was technology's next great opportunity. (Susan was not an immediate investor after the meeting; however, she came to help Arlan in time.)

After the conference, Arlan drafted an essay in *Medium*, "Dear White Venture Capitalists: If You're Reading This, It's (Almost!) Too Late," —which went viral. She challenged founders and VCs to reexamine their portfolios.

Therefore, if you haven't hired a team of people who are of color, female, and/or LGBT to actively turn over every stone, to scope out every nook and cranny, to pop out of every bush, to find every qualified underrepresented founder in this country, you're going to miss out on a lot of money when the rest of the investment world gets it.[34]

The post gave her the notoriety she needed and invitations poured in; however, the tone hadn't changed.

"I pitched to well-known VCs, and I was met with a pat on the head. 'Good idea, but let's talk another time,'" Hamilton

---

34 (Hamilton, 2015)

describes. "I thought, 'Cool. We'll talk when I'm writing a check across the table from you.'"[35]

Hamilton had built her confidence through relentless hustle. After pausing her music industry work in 2014, she battled periods of homelessness and financial struggle to pursue her venture. She worked every lead, contact, and made every cold call she could, eventually landing connections with Marc Andreessen (Netscape founder), Brad Field (Foundry Group), Stewart Butterfield (Flickr founder), and Aaron Levie (Box founder), to name a few who would become investors.

Asked how she built such an influential network she says, "It was seven days a week, 365 days, for three years of network building, being tenacious, and letting people see me over and over again."[36]

Today, Arlan's Backstage Capital has had more than $36 million in seed funding, of which they've invested—according to their website—"more than $4M in one hundred companies led by underrepresented founders."[37]

Their unique value, as described by Lars Rasmussen (an angel investor and former Googler) is, "She gets access to

---

35 (Rodriguez, 2016)
36 (Blodgett, 2017)
37 (Backstage Capital, 2018)

entrepreneurs that your typical Valley investor might not. It's almost like using an unfair advantage by knowing Arlan and using her connections into an area that is overlooked, and wrongly overlooked."

In the end, Arlan and Backstage are looking for the best, "This is not a nonprofit or a charity. I want killer companies that are making money and will make money. My job is to make money for my investors, and I can't do that with companies based on my heart. It has to be based on companies that are badass."[38]

UPSHOT

- **Being unusual can give you access to skills, views, and ideas that the "usual" don't have.**
- **Put yourself in the fray of new environments and then observe patterns.**
- **Become the unfair advantage.**

CULTIVATING GRIT

To master something hard, one needs a firmness of character, or grit. Can you cultivate it? The science says yes.

---

38   (Rodriguez, 2016)

Today's most notable expert on grit—thanks to an incredible, viral TED talk, is Angela Duckworth:

I think the misunderstanding—or, at least, one of them—is that it's only the perseverance part that matters. But I think the passion piece is at least as important. I mean, if you are really, really tenacious and dogged about a goal that's not meaningful to you, and not interesting to you—that's just drudgery. It's not just determination. It's having a direction that you care about.[39]

PASSION + PERSEVERANCE = GRIT

More recent studies support Duckworth's statement and go even further. According to Scott Barry Kaufman summarizing research for *Scientific American*:

Indeed, the findings...suggest that if we want to build grit, neither passion nor perseverance alone is enough. If you're just building perseverance, you're becoming better at being dutiful and resilient but may lose sight of the fact that what you are persevering toward really isn't personally meaningful. On the flipside, if you're just building passion, that's great, but all the passion in the world won't actually get it done (despite what commencement speakers might lead you to believe).[40]

---

39 (Duckworth, 2013)
40 (Kaufman, 2018)

Here's the special sauce, according to Kaufman:

The findings also suggest that an important source of grit is immersion or full absorption in a task relating to your long-term goals.[41]

Most people think of grit and they think of perseverance. What's important is to bring the passion and depth too.

* * *

"You wanna fly, you got to give up the shit that weighs you down."

—TONI MORRISON

Tess Holliday
How fucking hard I work.

"The reality is, that I was born to stand out," says Tess Holliday, plus-sized model, social media influencer, and body positivity activist.

---

41   (Kaufman, 2018)

"I was born to make people question things they thought they knew, and to exist fearlessly in a space that we are told bodies like mine don't deserve to be in."

This is a success Tess earned through years of work and learning, "My success has not been overnight. It's taken a long time to get here."

Born Ryann Maegen Hoven in 1985 in Mississippi, Tess experienced a tumultuous childhood: an adulterous father, constant moves, her parents' eventual divorce, and at age ten her mother's new boyfriend attempted to murder her mother by shooting her in the head, leaving her mother partially paralyzed. Tess and her younger brother moved in with their grandparents in a trailer in the backyard while their mother recovered.[42]

Tess became overweight in elementary school and faced bullying from her peers around her weight and family circumstances. By the time she was a teenager in the late 1990s, "I was getting shoved into lockers. I was being called names."[43]

Looking for a future and strength, she found inspiration the first time she saw plus-size models like Mia Tyler—and decided to try modeling at age fifteen.

42 (Holliday, 2017)
43 (Scott, 2018)

"I found out about plus-size modeling...and I went to an audition in Atlanta. They told me I was too short and I was too big, and I would never model. But I'm very hardheaded!" says Tess.[44]

Back home the bullying continued so intensely that she decided to drop out of school at age seventeen, eventually receiving her GED.

With her interest in fashion established, Tess relocated to Seattle in 2003 and became a makeup artist in addition to working part-time jobs in retail. She found work at fashion shows and expanded her skills into hair styling and directing.

Tess kept working on her own looks and enlisted friends to take pictures of her to post to websites.

"I had moved to Seattle. I had some photos taken by my boyfriend and posted to modeling website, Model Mayhem and forgot about it. I checked it about a year later [in 2010] and I had a message literally that day from a casting director for the A&E show "Heavy," which became my first job, to be the face of the show. Six months later I was on billboards and buses and every major magazine," says Tess.

---

44 (Okwodu, 2018)

Tess moved to Los Angeles for the show and doubled down on her brand and working as a model, without representation. She faced obstacles as a size twenty-two—the largest plus sized models at the time were size fourteen and sixteen, so she built a brand for herself on Instagram.

"It's definitely not a conventional route. Then again there's not really a conventional route in modeling." She became a social media maven, cultivating a following of one million on her own.[45]

In 2013 she garnered national attention after creating the viral hashtag #effyourbeautystandards, where she encouraged women of all sizes to reject regressive ideals. The campaign pushed her modeling career into the spotlight.

Just a year later, in 2014 she made history by becoming the first size-twenty-two model to be signed with a major agency, Milk Management—the signal that she had finally made it.[46]

Given all the obstacles she has faced, Tess regularly gets asked why she got into modeling.

"I didn't see anyone who looked like me...I mean look when I started. There were some girls on Tumblr out there and

45   (Torres, 2018)
46   (Peoples, 2016)

on Instagram and there still are. There's so many amazing body-positive bloggers and influencers out there that aren't getting the space they deserve. In the modeling world in particular there was no one past a size fourteen and unfortunately there's still not many people who are. I wanted to be that person—as unusual as that sounds. There's not as much diversity as I wish there was."[47]

In 2018, Tess set the goal to do high fashion—the exclusive high-end fashion with brands like Gucci, Vivienne Westwood, Yves St. Laurant etc. This includes photo shoots and also runway shows in brands that do not sell to plus-size customers.

A member of her team told her it would be impossible. And she fired them. Later that year she was invited to walk in two high-fashion runways and made it on the covers of *Cosmopolitan* and *People* magazines. "When people tell me I can't do something, it makes me want to do it," says Tess.[48]

"I think I have a career because I never gave up. I had to fight for everything. I was always in a position where I had to figure things out on my own. So when people told me I couldn't model, I just remember thinking it was ridiculous. I felt like I had already been through the impossible."

---

47   (Torres, 2018)
48   (Tempesta, 2018)

Sometimes getting through the impossible in our personal lives prepares us for the impossible in our work lives.

"I know I have selling power. I know people like seeing bigger bodies and marginalized bodies because I represent women you don't see a lot in media and in print," she explains.[49]

"It would just be nice," she says, "if people acknowledged how fucking hard I work."[50]

UPSHOT

- **Your difference represents consumers and customers. Even if they aren't getting noticed.**
- **Follow the desire to do something even as the Only.**

ACTION ITEMS FOR CAREER DOMINATION

MINDSET

I will transmute my struggle into skills. It is easy to become focused on the pain we feel during struggle. Notice the pain. Then shift your attention and focus to what you are doing to navigate that struggle. You can focus on the people, industry, or products that inspire you more than the pain that

---

49 IBD
50 (Hazlehurst, 2018)

hurts. Look at the activities that keep you going and get the job done.

Parlay your skills. This is the ultimate tactic to change jobs, careers, roles within your organization, or make the leap from employee to business owner. Revisit the list of skills you drafted in the last chapter. Now expand it to every single skill you use on a daily basis. This could be as simple as "types sixty words per minute" to "influences teams of junior staff in unconventional ways and they are..." and be thorough. Which skills are useful beyond your current job/role/or occupation?

In what environments do you want to be? Ask yourself who you want to be surrounded by and why? Do you have a desire to be in a place you are not but fear there is no one like you there? If you did not judge your desire to be in that environment/industry/type of work, what elements attract you to that space or the people in it? Define this.

PART 2

ENERGIZE

[animate; enliven; spark; turn on; activate; excite]

Developing and pursuing your high-level professional path as an Other requires a strong engine. This is the Part where we mobilize towards the environments in which we want to be.

Get pumped up!

CHAPTER 4

HURRICANE FORCE WOMEN

———

"It's not people's backgrounds that make them successful. It's their psychology; it's their mindset. It's do they have a way of consistently focusing, obsessing about something so important to them and do they have a way to make it happen?"

—TONY ROBBINS

You can feel their being as much as see it.

Everyone who meets one of them wants to either: 1) be her best friend 2) work for her or 3) buy her a drink.

Often times all three.

These women are the Hurricane Force Women.

And we all have one within us.

* * *

Talls
Human Exhilaration.

The thing about someone with a grand presence is that they influence you through their being. There's actually this sensation when they leave a room where things become so quiet and empty you can feel a small pang of sadness. That energy and aliveness (just like Elvis!) has left the building.

It's dramatic for a second.

My Aunt Lorian has that presence.

If you looked up the definition of "Life of the Party" in the dictionary, you would see "Kate's Aunt Lorian." She's someone to whom everyone gravitates at any party or gathering of any group of one+ people. This woman is so vivacious, energetic, loud, and positive, she practically radiates *thirst for life* as she bounces from person to activity.

Her technical nickname is "Talls" because when her late husband Edward saw her at their first party and wanted to ask her for a date, he asked her friend, "Who was that tall girl who laughed a lot?"

At work Lorian is a Fortune 500 Director.

You would never know it meeting her on the weekend; she does a thorough job of "removing her suit" on Fridays. Edward always insisted she turn off her work email and cell phone on the weekend.

To boot, she never finished college.

This is a rarity. A typical qualification for Director level is at least a bachelor's degree and an MBA, and often from a top program. Furthermore, [Cite- working mother] recent data reveals that just one in ten profit and loss positions—or line jobs—at Fortune 500 companies are held by women.

Yet Lorian is humble.

She started her career with her company as a blue collar worker and never had just one "big break" into white collar work. Rather she had a slow and steady progression through the company over decades. It was not a sexy rise and she was never gunning for a top job.

It is impossible to distinguish which is more attractive: Talls' verve as a *human* or her role as a powerful private sector leader.

Lost in much of our diversity discussions—especially in the framing of injustices, abuses of power, and poor leadership—are the dynamos who are raising the frequency of the room. They walk in high on life and can best any asshole. It's not about business tactics or privilege. It's about *internal force.*

I see hurricane force women as flying above and over challenges.

* * *

vi·brant

/ˈvībrənt/

adjective

1. full of energy and enthusiasm[51]

Is vibrancy actually an advantage? In fact, yes.

---

51   Merriam-Webster, s.v. "vibrant," accessed June 15, 2019, https://www.merriam-webster.com/dictionary/vibrant.

In 1980, CBS reporter Morley Safer attended a three-day seminar in Dallas, Texas, where Ed Foreman taught everyday people how to gain an edge in the workforce.[52]

The secret sauce? Enthusiasm.

Ed Foreman, a motivational speaker and the only two-time congressman in two states in the last one hundred years, claimed he could make individuals richer, better and happier just by changing their mindset from "a frightened little church mouse" to that of a "super mouse."[53]

During the seminar, Safer reports, *"Some advice was as simple as answering, "Terrific!" when asked, "How are you?" Other advice included filling out goal planners and a creative ideas manual. Foreman's gospel and that of his competitor, Zig Ziglar (referred to as the "most fantastic man outside of God" by a loyal follower), earned both men millions."*

Safer was baffled by the simplicity of the seminars and asked Ed if he was simply stating the obvious when he preached *"life is for laughing, loving, and living."*

Ed's response, *"Well, it might be the obvious, but very few people, in fact, in life practice it..."*

---

52 (Safer, 2014)
53 IBD

"A positive mental attitude and action plus a specific, identifiable, written goal equals supper on the table, equals health, wealth and happiness."[54]

You can be one of the few.

* * *

"My mother always told me—and I thought this was genius—there are a lot of inequalities in the world. Be so outstanding that there is no debate."

—CARLA HARRIS

Carla Harris
When you tell me I can't do something, I'm all over it.

"If you want an A, shoot for the A+, so if the teacher is unfair, you still get an A," says Carla Harris, Vice Chairman and Managing Director at Morgan Stanley on her upbringing.

This lens defined her early education and launch in her career.

---

54 IBD

"I grew up as an only child in a no-nonsense, no-excuses household. My parents gave me the sense that I was supposed to do well and never made me think it was extraordinary to get A's or to excel in school. I remember telling my father, 'You owe me money for my A' because one of my classmates was getting paid every time she got a good grade in school. But my father said, 'I don't owe you anything. That's what you're supposed to do.'"[55]

* * *

Growing up in Jacksonville, Florida, Carla attended some of the best schools in the area and gained admission to Harvard University in 1980. In her initial days at Harvard, she took some introductory classes to explore possible majors. Looking for advice from a teaching fellow, he told her, "Girl, whatever you do, don't major in economics."[56]

The advice bothered her, "When it was time to declare [my] major, I went straight to the dean and wrote down 'economics.' I'm negatively motivated. When you tell me I can't do something, I'm all over it."[57]

---

55 (Zarya, 2016)
56 (Leibowitz, 2018)
57 IBD

Carla graduated Magna Cum Laude in Economics in 1984, clearly all over it.

She had also spent time exploring her career options, "I had no idea I wanted to do finance. Growing up black in the south, if you were smart, people pushed you into one of three primary lanes: 1) to be a doctor or a nurse 2) to be a teacher or 3) to be a lawyer. It wasn't until after my sophomore year of college that I had exposure to finance and to Wall Street."

During her undergraduate work, Carla had considered a legal career until she learned more about finance and gained clarity. "I realized the things that attracted me to the law were actually found in business: 1) I wanted to have a lot of responsibility very early on 2) I wanted to be in a position to call the shots around important issues and 3) I wanted to have a certain lifestyle, i.e. make a lot of money."

Harvard Business School welcomed her for an MBA after completing her bachelor's in 1984. She continued to consider a Wall Street career. "The other thing that piqued my interest and probably pushed me over the edge [for a career in finance] was the fact that I did not see a lot of people who looked like me. I didn't see a lot of people of color. I didn't see a lot of women. And I'm negatively motivated."[58]

---

58   (Harris, 2018)

After graduation, Harris joined Morgan Stanley as an associate in mergers and acquisitions (M&A). "Frankly, the reason I chose M&A was around the negative motivation. Everyone told me, 'Don't do M&A' because they don't have a life. They're always on call. It's a miserable existence. So I said, 'aha,' I've gotta do M&A. I knew if it was that busy and it had that kind of deal flow and that kind of deal volume, I would learn the most in the shortest period of time."[59]

That decision to join mergers and acquisitions was strategic and successful. Carla went on to lead the M&A group and eventually Morgan Stanley globally.

Her meteoric rise at the organization prompted her to write several books, codifying her career knowledge into "Carla's Pearls of Wisdom," which she now shares through speaking engagements around the world.[60]

* * *

HOW PEOPLE DESCRIBE YOU WHEN
YOU ARE NOT IN THE ROOM

"Coming out of college and business school, I embraced the concept of a meritocracy, which suggests that you just need

59 (Leibowitz, 2018)
60 (Harris, 2019)

to be smart and work hard. But after starting my career, I realized there were other things that informed the success equation, like understanding that perception is the copilot to reality," says Carla Harris.[61]

"Every company says that if you do really good work, if you keep your head down, you will go right to the top. But nobody ever takes the time to explain the nuances of how that work gets viewed or graded."

"All major decisions about your career will be made when you are not in the room. How do you want people to describe you when you aren't in the room? Pick three adjectives that really describe who you are. Authenticity is important. However, pick three adjectives that are also valued in your organization."

In Carla's world, it's important to be seen as tough. She remembers an "aha" moment early in her career on Wall Street when a senior manager said, "You're smart, you work hard, but you're not tough enough for this business."

Harris was taken aback. She knew she was tough—really tough. Tough enough to be successful on Wall Street.

---

61 (Marcus, 2016)

"The last thing you want to be thought of as a woman on Wall Street is not tough," Harris said. "I realized the real Carla Harris was not walking into Morgan Stanley every day… it was creating a competitive disadvantage for me. For ninety days, I would walk tough, talk tough, eat tough, drink tough. You must have consistent behavior around those four adjectives."

Harris says she often critiqued management presentations at work and one day, when a colleague asked her to come listen to a CEO's presentation, she realized her acting "tough" had paid off.

"I said, 'Tell me about this CEO. Does he have thick skin? Because I'm tough,'" she said.[62]

UPSHOT

- **Be so outstanding there is no debate.** Easier said than done—more a journey than destination. This is one of the most critical endeavors on the road to success when you're different.
- **If someone says you can't do something, reduce them to the heckler to your act.** You've challenged that person's comfort level; they'd prefer you to keep things as

---

62 (Burns, 2014)

they are. Do what any good entertainer would do with a heckler. Use their attention and comments to fuel your performance.

- **Research and clarify the key adjectives of successful people at your organization.** Do you embody the traits you discover? What behaviors are rewarded?

* * *

"There are years that ask questions and years that answer."
—ZORA NEALE HURSTON

Jessica Matthews
The Thing Is That We're Not Often Told Young People Are The Ones Likely To Change The World.

"Very much me, I felt like I have lived this life of un-likelies."

The first time I read this astounding biography I had to read it again: *dual degrees from Harvard, including an MBA, listings on over ten patents and patents pending, inclusions on both* Forbes *30 under 30,* Inc. Magazine *30 under 30, and awarded Harvard Scientist of the Year. [This person] founded their current company at age twenty-two and was invited by President*

Barack Obama to the White House to represent small compa-
nies for the signing of the America Invents Act in 2012.[63]

This is the description of Jessica O. Matthews, who in 2011 founded the company Uncharted Power, whose mission is to, "…use our renewable kinetic energy solutions to generate clean, consistent, and cost-efficient power for communities, facilities, and the Internet of Things."[64]

In 2008, at the age of nineteen, Jessica invented the Soccket, a soccer ball that harnesses kinetic energy (generated by the ball's motion) to provide reliable off-grid power. The Soccket has made an impact replacing generators and kerosene lamps in villages in developing nations where infrastructure is unreliable. According to Jessica, "There are two billion people in the world without access to reliable electricity who could benefit from Uncharted's work."[65] The invention has expanded solutions to vehicular, lifestyle, and pedestrian solutions—think strollers, carts, sidewalks, anything that moves or people move next to or on.

"For me that story started in Poughkeepsie, New York (the same place where Snookie from Jersey Shore is from). It's not the most inspiring place. I'm a dual citizen of Nigeria

---

63 (Power, 2018)
64 IBD
65 (Aspen Institute, 2016)

and the US; both of my parents are from Nigeria and met in Brooklyn. They pushed me to believe in what I can do, but growing up in Poughkeepsie I didn't get to see a lot of opportunities beyond what I knew. I did see the American Dream and also the challenges my family living in Nigeria faced."[66]

Jessica showed academic promise in public school without extra resources. "We didn't have a great school system in Poughkeepsie and I didn't go to a Phillips Exeter, but I was somehow able to get myself into Harvard."

Jessica emphasizes often that she was not an engineering or even a science major at Harvard [2006-2010]. "Studying Psychology and Economics (not Engineering), I went into a special course 'Idea Translation: Affecting Change Through Art and Science.' They asked us to come up with a problem and then a unique solution combining art and science. I was thinking I'm not an artist and definitely not a scientist, save my love of Bill Nye the Science Guy. I started thinking about my experiences in Nigeria seeing the actual need for power, seeing the actual problem first-hand. There are nearly two billion people on this planet living without reliable access to electricity. They end up using either a diesel generator or a kerosene lamp."[67]

---

66 IBD
67 IBD

The class and problem intrigued her. "I said, I may not be a scientist, but I do have a meaningful bank of experiences that would be worthwhile to pursue...on top of the energy issue I found there was an incredible love [in the developing world] of soccer. I thought what if I could combine the two."

She often gets asked how she learned the complex science needed to invent the Soccket, "How did I teach myself mechanical and electrical engineering? Google and Wikipedia...I started to sketch out ideas I remembered from basic physics class. Not even honors physics, just basic physics!"

Mentally Jessica kept her fears in check during the process, telling herself, "How could someone who is not an engineer and does not play soccer develop this? And really it was just a question of, 'Why not?' The cool thing of starting young and just pushing is that you have nothing to lose. At the very least you have an amazing failure to talk about in your college essay. At best you create something the world has never seen. And that's how I kept on pushing. I also listened to a lot of Beyoncé while I was working."[68]

---

68 IBD

YOUTH IS A GROWING ADVANTAGE

For a long time, young people have gotten a bad rap. They've been judged as aimless, restless, and often reckless.

Times are changing—as impacts of globalization and technology combine, young people are feeling more empowered to shape the world.

As Noa Gafni of the World Economic Forum reports, "According to the National Careers Service, 70% of young people want to find a career that changes the world for the better. Meanwhile, ethics as a motivation for buying things has risen 26% since 2008 (Edelman), and 84% of Millennials consider it their duty to improve the world, says a report from Deloitte."[69]

As technology makes the world increasingly one global village, young people are quickly and easily connecting around the world—and using it to tackle complex problems.

"From the United States to Sierra Leone, young people are taking matters in their own hands to make an impact. They think governments are slow and usually incapable of tackling complex challenges that need immediate solutions. That is why they are working with each other, at times experimenting

---

69 (Gafni, 2014)

and failing, to tackle problems," says Ravi Kumal, digital strategist at The World Bank.[70]

Not so aimless, really.

* * *

The natural assumption is Jessica Matthews needed a lot of technology and capital to develop the complex Soccket. "When I get asked how did you acquire the resources to produce the Soccket, I say 'hustle, hustle, hustle.' You don't have to be that wealthy...you'd be surprised how much innovation can come from $100. A lot of the early prototypes of the Soccket were made from materials from Duane Read and Rite Aid stores."[71]

Jessica formed Uncharted Power (originally Uncharted Play) in 2011 officially, after a brief stint with another start-up upon graduation. "I realized that when you're doing something innovative there's no real way to be taught how to do it. You just have to have the courage to struggle, fall down, and get back up."[72]

---

70 (World Bank, 2016)
71 (Institute, 2016)
72 IBD

Today the company has distributed products around the world and is working with Fortune 100 companies to integrate their technology into a plethora of products.

"It all came from me looking at who I am and where I come from and instead of seeing that as an obstacle, seeing that as a competitive advantage...an opportunity to see the world in a way that other people don't see it. And making something out of it," says Jessica.[73]

Through her success in making the most of minimal resources, Jessica's intelligence and savvy in launching Uncharted Power caught the eye of investors. She currently holds the record for largest Series A funding ever raised by a black female founder, $7 million.[74]

This accomplishment is impressive and also a rarity. To date, only a few dozen black women have raised more than $1 million in venture capital funding. Thus there is a unique pressure on black female founders. As Jessica says, "Whenever you are a black face in a white space, your presence represents all black people. You don't have the ability to be flawed. Any mistake you make will be the one data point to explain an entire people."[75]

---

73 IBD
74 (Klich, 2018)
75 (Harris, 2018)

Nonetheless, Jessica's verve continues to drive Uncharted Power to new heights as an organization. She seemingly cannot be limited or contained.

UPSHOT

- **Inspiration can come from the unlikeliest of places.** If you are an Unlikely, you know the process of digging, reaching, and pushing on seemingly less resources than those around you.
- **Embrace the "recklessness" of youth.** All that energy just needs a channel.
- **Seeing the world in a way others do not can be a competitive advantage.** This is the epitome of "fresh perspective."

All three women here have been anointed a grand title, "Hurricane Force Women." While they are very different as individuals and backgrounds, they share a verve and unrelenting spirit that has taken them to the top. Through a variety of tools and approaches, they blow past adversity.

ACTION ITEMS FOR CAREER DOMINATION

MINDSET

Negative motivation is my secret weapon in the face of adversity. Keep track of every comment, statement, and problem people throw at you that either says or implies, "You can't do X." Write it on a piece of paper, in a journal, or other preferred medium and refer regularly. Compile and slay.

EXERCISE

Get your playlists. For Lorian it was funk, for Carla it was gospel, and for Jessica it was Beyoncé. They all had Force Music in their lives that they religiously listened to that gave them power. Identify the music that gets you fired up about your business and play it as a practice. At the office. In the airport. While you're doing dishes. All of the above.

Get your freebies. The free resources for education now available are mind-blowing. Identify three major websites and tools with the knowledge you need that you don't have right now. Credentialing and education are easier than ever.

CHAPTER 5

OUT BY DESIGN: CHALLENGING CONVENTION

———

"And there you have our difference: to be in hell is to drift, to be in heaven is to steer."

—GEORGE BERNARD SHAW

Who you are is powerful.

How does that play into what you are going to do?

INTERVIEW RESILIENCE

There was this time when I applied for a recruiting job with a small company. They invited me to interview with a smattering of people from their talent team and administration. The CEO was not on my agenda, so you can imagine my surprise when he walked in halfway through my day—and during an interview—to see if we could chat for fifteen minutes. The person I was interviewing with complied and hustled out, just as shocked as me at his arrival.

In typical CEO-fashion, this gentleman commenced to pepper me with highly skeptical and blunt questions, beginning with:

"So, you here slumming it with us after your time with the big boys?"

Fantastic. You had me at jackass.

I took the high road, "I'm here because I need something different. I've done my time at the big organizations and am ready to be somewhere I can have a meaningful impact."

He rolled with it, seemingly satisfied. He tried a few more short questions before launching on a soliloquy about his organizational challenges (which turns out were pretty riveting). I was intrigued. Two minutes later from him:

"Kate, we need people who are resilient here. Are you resilient?"

Am I resilient? What the hell kind of interview question is that?

Rule number one: never ask a yes/no question of an interviewee. In what hypothetical would a candidate ever answer "no" and expect good things?

I felt intense emotion in that moment. I clammed up and felt unusually angry. Something was going to spill out of me—the thing I wanted to say—instead of the thing I was supposed to say. I fought it for a few minutes but felt empowered by how much of a jerk he had been to me up to that moment. What did I have to lose? This company could kiss my ass. So I went there.

"Well I'm a lesbian. Of course I'm resilient."

He had a stuttered cough and then came back.

"Well, how does being a lesbian make you more resilient than anyone else?" he asked.

Without pause I explained, "It's a miracle I'm sitting in front of you today. I've had to face losing the love of those who mattered most to me."

He kept talking and somehow (in a helpful, less jackass-sort-of-way) brought us back to the topic of the company.

That was the first time I had ever come out of the closet in an interview. It was risky, uncomfortable, and I could not believe I was doing it so unapologetically.

And then the offer came just days after that interview.

* * *

Coming out is an incredibly personal decision. My general rule is that everyone should refrain from coming out in interviews for the same reasons you should refrain from talking about your family or personal relationships no matter who you are. It's irrelevant to whether you can perform the job duties or not. Why take a chance on losing out because of bias you cannot control? You want to keep the focus of the discussion on you as a professional (whoever you are) and not on your personal life.

Then again, you can *gain power* by establishing and owning your identity from the outset.

This is a delicate and bold move. One which must be done right.

I challenged my own conventions by coming out in that interview.

* * *

pow·er

/ˈpaú(-ə)r /

noun

1: ability to act or produce an effect
2: possession of control, authority, or influence over others
3: physical might[76]

On the most basic level, power skills and behavior matter significantly to career success, and this is backed by research.

According to Stanford Graduate School of Business professor, Jeffrey Pfeffer:

It's not just women or Asian Americans who sometimes have trouble doing things such as advocating for themselves and their accomplishments, negotiating for salary and job

---

76 Merriam-Webster, s.v. "power," accessed June 15, 2019, https://www. merriam-webster.com/dictionary/power

responsibilities rather than just accepting what employers offer, networking, and not obsessively worrying about being liked—all things that bring increased power. Many people are uncomfortable with power and the behaviors required to obtain it.[77]

A great example of this research includes studies by professors at Cornell University in the late 1990s, who tested political influence behaviors in jobs and found:

Results from a sample of past graduates of two universities indicated that supervisor-focused tactics, manifesting a strategy of ingratiation, resulted in higher levels of career success while job-focused tactics, manifesting a strategy of self-promotion, resulted in lower levels of success.[78]

As Pfeffer describes:

Contrary to what you may think, good job performance is not going to be enough to rocket your career ahead. After all, the numerous studies that show salary and promotions are affected by things such as race and gender, educational credentials, and years of experience—none of which are dimensions of job performance—make the point that the world is

---

77 (Pfeffer, 2015)
78 (Judge & Bretz, 2005)

not always a just and fair place and it takes more than doing
a good job to be successful.[79]

Power is pivotal to your career success, and it is something
you can absolutely obtain.

* * *

"People who allow their situations and other people to change
who they are each die having been many people."

—MOKOKOMA MOKHONOANA

Micah Gellman
What I Created Rather Than What I Thought
They Wanted.

Looking at Micah Gellman's background, you'd never guess
he wasn't a square. Totally conventional success: top Manhattan high school, Harvard University undergrad, McKinsey
& Company.

On paper, he appears accomplished, put-together, and adept
at doing "all the right things." Most people would applaud

---

79   (Pfeffer, 2015)

his success or feel envy because he is a member of many elite groups.

The person behind the profile is a different story.

Growing up in a household with divorced parents, Micah describes, "I saw the void of traditional masculine leader of the house and stepped in to assume it." He spent much of his adolescence working to appear to have all facets of the image and pushing down his feelings to the contrary.

"I was very aware of what was prestigious and impressive." Micah focused on those values in high school through strong grades, test scores, musical achievements, and building friendships. By 2011, his senior year of high school, he was ready to apply to top universities, especially Yale.

"I crafted a sophisticated application for early admission [indicating to the school he was committed to attending if accepted], and waited to hear back."

The response from Yale: deferral.

This was not a flat-out no, more a strong maybe. Yet Micah had a strong reaction.

"I had a huge wake-up call. I realized I had crafted a persona and it wasn't working. I realized I was miserable and that early admission wouldn't mollify my feelings of discontent."

Micah describes that he then "opened the door to [his] inner self." Shortly thereafter he started the process of coming out of the closet—which launched a "two-year journey of healing and discovery"—and took some bold steps to prepare himself for the challenging process of regular college admissions applications with only a few months to make adjustments. Acceptance rates are typically lower in regular decision period than early decision.

Micah pivoted his essays—the most personal part of his application—and chose to be as honest and authentic as he could. "I changed all of my essays from something rigorous and standard about music and my piano experience—which revealed nothing about me—to whimsical pieces about the NYC subway."

His strategy was to focus on "what I created rather than what I thought they wanted." Emboldened by the feelings of freedom that came with writing what he had seen in the world, through his own queer, artistic lens and having to try new things, he bravely presented himself to colleges as *Micah*.

It worked.

He was accepted to all of the other top universities to which he applied: the full Ivy League (Brown, Columbia, Dartmouth, etc.), Duke, and Stanford. Micah reflects on his early time in high school as "successful pretending" until he discovered even more success as the person he naturally expressed.

Oh and Yale still turned him down. "I'll never know why I was not accepted there."

POWER SKILLS

"Building power and influence skills is not about changing who you are or becoming someone else. It is about adding a set of activities and skills to your repertoire to become more effective and successful," says Jeffrey Pfeffer

What activities and skills does he recommend?

1. Networking: *spend more time building social relationships.*
2. Building Personal Qualities: *energy, the ability to tolerate conflict, the capacity to see others' points of view and interests, resilience, and ambition, among others, are qualities that produce power.*
3. Learn How to Act and Speak with Power: *body language is important because we form impressions of others quickly and then subsequently assimilate information based on*

these first impressions. Use emotion-producing, vivid language and stories to convey your message. Use forceful, powerful gestures. Speak loudly and don't raise your voice at the end of statements, implying a question rather than an assertion.

4. Challenge Convention: *Understand and then act on the insight that particularly if you are an underdog, breaking the rules—which are, after all, mostly set by those in power—is essential to winning.*[80]

We've explored networking, building personal qualities, and acting and speaking with power in previous chapters. So let's talk more about challenging convention.

WEIRD INFLUENCE

So what choice do you make when you've been accepted to all of the great schools for university? You take a year off [and later attend Harvard].

Micah saved all of his money from odd jobs to spend a year in Latin America reflecting, integrating, and finding his grounding. "I would hop online at a local internet cafe about once a week but otherwise I was off the grid."

---

80 (Pfeffer, 2015)

While others felt pressured to follow that path (the one where you don't take breaks on the hamster wheel), Micah relished the pause.

It impacted his experience at Harvard when he finally arrived in 2013 and witnessed the immediate pressure and culture to join clubs and be a leader on campus. "That did not resonate with me, so I did not hop on that bandwagon. Instead, I looked for major issues that weren't being addressed by student groups and rallied new organizations or improvements on the old."

At first, Micah did not have a strategy for his own social impact on campus or who he wanted to be. "I did not identify as an entrepreneur. Rather, I was just different from the norms around me."

He found himself invigorated by the idea of "making groups or organizations weirder. They tended to be very straight and narrow." Something inside of Micah resonated in situations where he could inspire difference or a new way of thinking rather than being a member of a group to keep the organization running.

This paid off. "I eventually influenced a historic all-male social club to open up membership to all genders"—a true reflection of how Micah saw the impact of difference. When asked how he accomplished such a feat he says, "People are more receptive to change than you might think but often get mired in the process. I kept the group focused on the impact of making the change."

In the back of Micah's mind throughout his undergraduate experience, he kept wondering, "How do I translate this to a career?" Just like his attraction to influencing social clubs in new ways, Micah was more drawn to unique experiences.

"I looked hard at unconventional opportunities: fellowships, scholarships, working with underprivileged children abroad, hell, even farming in rural France." While his peers were focused on large companies, traditional graduate programs such as JDs., and MBAs, Micah had a hard time seeing himself in corporate America. "It was too conventional."

In his senior year at Harvard in 2016—and on a whim—he applied to McKinsey & Company. It seemed a long shot, given his résumé. In fact, Micah thought he didn't have the résumé of a future consultant. "I didn't do anything in college that screamed consulting or even business."

At first he was declined a campus interview but was able to land an interview when a last-minute spot opened up.

Surprisingly for Micah, he hit it off with all of his interviewers and could see himself with the firm. "They were solving problems all over the world in ways I was excited about." When McKinsey extended Micah an offer, he felt validated for presenting himself honestly during interviews, "I was super open about who I am and did not present a persona I thought they wanted to see."

Today Micah travels the US and the globe as a consultant, gainfully employed.

"To me it's so weird that I've been attracted to management consulting. For me it was the unconventional choice."

UPSHOT

- **Follow your wake-up calls.** Wake-up calls are the messages from the deepest reaches of our brains and/or hearts guiding us through blocks. Oftentimes we are asleep at the wheel or fearful of acknowledging our beliefs and behaviors that are ineffective.
- **Stop crafting personas.** This is the truth behind the advice "bring your whole self to work." People have amazing bullshit detectors—even if you think you're putting on a strong act. Ultimately, you cannot reach your full potential when you hold yourself back.

- **Organizations need the unconventional—as does one's career.** Your weirdness is your road map.

✳ ✳ ✳

"When you become the image of your own imagination, it's the most powerful thing you could ever do."

—RUPAUL

Fiona Grant
I actually benefited from being different.

"I'm one of those Gen Xers who stayed with the same company for life," says Fiona Grant, a former Managing Director with global professional services firm, Accenture. She had a noticeably positive experience with Accenture—as a leader and an out lesbian for the majority of her tenure.

Originally joining the London office in 1989, the large, youthful office made her feel welcome. "My colleagues were so tuned-in to who I was. Some knew my partner had moved to the UK from the US, and I came out in the office gradually through the early 1990s." It finally came to a head in 1995, when a senior partner called her into his office to ask why she had not disclosed her partner to everybody. Rather than making her fear, the "outing" felt like moral support and boosted her confidence to disclose her personal life formally.

Fiona started out as a consultant and flourished with the organization, getting exposure to recruiting and change management before homing in on human resources as her focus.

With an American life partner, Fiona eyed moving to the United States in the mid 1990s for their relationship—to be closer to her partner's parents—although she harbored concerns that she wouldn't be able to be out about her relationship in the US.

In 1996, a human resources manager role with a new internal group opened up in the Washington, DC office—the right next role for her career. She was able to approach Accenture to sponsor a work visa and the firm was supportive of the move and her family.

Still, Fiona had reservations. "It is funny to look back and think how I assumed Washington, D.C. would be stuffy; with everyone wearing the obligatory yellow tie!"

As she arrived, a senior finance leader and out gay man, Richard, approached her. "On only the second day of my arrival, he outed and informally adopted me as his mentee and friend. We became tight-knit from then on and worked closely together on LGBT initiatives in the office." Again the patronage boosted Fiona's confidence in Accenture's support of her, inspiring her boldness to put herself out there within the company.

Her self-awareness at work, which led to notoriety and respect from her colleagues, only strengthened when she became a parent. In 1999, "My wife and I decided to become parents, and becoming a parent is a huge normalization."

Accustomed to having a different lens than her straight colleagues, her foray into parenting endeared her with her colleagues and earned her power. She became emboldened to take more of a stand for her communities and drove the effort with a small team to "make the business case for domestic partner benefits at Accenture," with the CEO.

The team was successful and Accenture chose to implement the benefits, additionally supporting the creation of an Employee Resource Group (ERG) to ensure a national network for LGBTQ employees.

From there, Fiona continued to be a champion and leader within the organization."I always volunteered to be the diversity lead on initiatives. Eventually I was easy to recognize by colleagues because I had been in so many internal ERG videos."

Over time, Fiona had been progressively promoted to a Human Resources Senior Manager and eventually senior roles with global influence and oversight on Diversity & Inclusion Initiatives. As she earned recognition and responsibilities, "I actually benefited from being different in terms of promotions, as once you get beyond the manager ranks, you need to have traits that differentiate yourself." Fiona developed a reputation for being "an authentic leader" and says, "I knew I was promoted partly because I was open about my sexuality, and that I had coached and mentored others going through the same experiences."

UPSHOT

- **Lean in to being outed, whoever you are.** When you take full ownership for who you are as a political maneuver—as much as personal acceptance—you gain momentum in your pursuits. People also align their impressions of you with what you demonstrate to them; the harmony resonates for building trust, confidence, and rapport.
- **Some environments are more welcoming than others; keep searching for the ones that are.** Fiona blazed a trail to ensure that the others who came behind her have

critical workplace rights and benefits. Never settle for organizations below the bar.

- **Being different from your peers can actually be the distinction you need to move into higher levels in an organization.** By connecting with members of your staff/workforce/group who are outside the usual, you mobilize resources for the organization that might otherwise be untapped or uncultivated.

ACTION ITEMS FOR CAREER DOMINATION

MINDSET

I am me, and I am here to deliver extraordinary value. The more unique your heritage, background, experiences, or personal intersections the better. Focus on what you will produce, deliver, or contribute to environments that no one else can. Notice the shift from debating who you are to you to producing what you specially can.

EXERCISE

Create opportunities specifically to have the ear of someone powerful. Highly successful people are not only prepared for these moments. They create them.

1. Join boards.

2. Volunteer for projects at work. Especially risky or new ones.
3. Look for ways to help others. Eventually people at the top will notice—really.
4. Cultivate cold contacting interesting people outside of your immediate network as a regular practice. Countless email templates and guides are written on this.

Come to all key interactions with questions (usually five to ten) every time. This applies to informational interviews, introductory conversations, formal interviews, meetings with people more senior than you, and those more junior than you. Do your homework ahead of time so that the questions glean new information to you and reveal to the person that you care.

PART 3

ENGAGE

[immerse; face; take on; battle; absorb]

New opportunities always arrive. Prepare for them and leverage your toolkit when they do. There is no room for sitting on the sidelines.

Sometimes you will need to fight. Sometimes you will need to trust.

CHAPTER 6

OPPORTUNITY TO TRUST

———

"Not knowing when the dawn will come, I open every door."

—EMILY DICKINSON

Opportunities are presenting themselves.

Are you ready to engage?

HIGH STAKES COMPETITION

In early 2018, IBM filed a lawsuit against an exiting employee, claiming that person's departure to join a competitor violated a one-year non-compete agreement.

Large companies like IBM file lawsuits regularly; this could have been a run-of-the-mill story. In fact, non-compete agreements are standard business practice in many organizations for healthy reasons. They protect companies from the unfair damage caused by an employee having inside information.

However, what's interesting about this story is the plaintiff involved was Lindsay-Rae McIntyre, IBM's Chief Diversity Officer and VP of Human Resources, and she had accepted the role of Chief Diversity Officer with Microsoft. She had spent almost twenty years with IBM.

Companies almost never sue HR or People Executives in this way. And the media noticed.

Geekwire reported, "The suit...describes McIntyre as one of the company's 'most senior executives with knowledge of IBM's most closely guarded and competitively sensitive strategic plans and recruitment initiatives,' including 'confidential strategies to recruit, retain and promote diverse talent.'"[81]

Chris Dolmetsch, of *Bloomberg* wrote, "...a case that elevates recruiting and promotion of an inclusive workforce to the level of safeguarding proprietary technology." He further wrote:

---

81   (Bishop, 2018)

Technology and financial companies have reserved those fights in the past to employees who possessed key technical or strategic knowledge, not those entrusted to make decisions on hiring and the makeup of the workforce. … McIntyre oversaw teams responsible for developing artificial intelligence-based tools and methods used to track career development, recommend growth and promotion opportunities and measure diversity metrics, IBM said.[82]

Staff reporters for Gartner described the profundity of the story. "This particular case is actually rather flattering to the practice of diversity and inclusion in general as it shines a light on the increasing role that diversity measures play in corporate America."[83]

We're now in an era when the ability to recruit and retain diverse employees can be a significant competitive advantage for businesses—so much so they're willing to sue for it.

* * *

---

82   (Staff, 2018)
83   IBD

trust

\ ˈtrəst \

noun

1a: assured reliance on the character, ability, strength, or truth of someone or something
b: one in which confidence is placed
2a: dependence on something future or contingent: HOPE[84]

Every year, the public relations firm Edelman releases the results of its global survey on public trust. The survey is large, usually encompassing tens of thousands of respondents in twenty to thirty countries. Edelman measures attitudes regarding the state of trust in media, government, nonprofits, and business.

According to the 2019 report, from 2018 to 2019, the United States saw the largest decrease in trust in all institutions of any country surveyed. In fact, 46 percent of US respondents believe "the system is failing me." And it's no surprise in a

---

84 Merriam-Webster, s.v. "power," accessed June 15, 2019, https://www.merriam-webster.com/dictionary/power

polarized political climate that only 48 percent of US respondents "trust government."[85]

Yet 75 percent "trust my employer."[86]

Not all employers are the same or even worthy of our trust. But I take that national high confidence in employers overall as a positive sign.

To take risks, show enthusiasm, and be themselves, one must be able to trust those who hold the power.

* * *

"There is a special place in hell for women who don't help each other."

—MADELEINE ALBRIGHT

Cindy Robbins
Comfortable with being uncomfortable.

Over twelve years, the Chief People Officer of Salesforce, Cindy Robbins, built a position of clout that allowed her to

---

85   (Ries et al., 2018)
86   IBD

influence its gender pay gap and overall tone toward minorities in a tremendous way.

As one of the largest (thirty thousand employees worldwide) and most influential companies in Silicon Valley (and recently ranked by *Fortune* as one of the top places in the US to work) the impact of the change has inspired far and wide.

In 1994, Cindy moved to San Francisco after graduating from Santa Clara University. At the time she found a plethora of opportunities in the tech sector. "I went back and forth from sales and recruiting and finally back into recruiting, and made it through the dotcom boom" working at a variety of small companies for ten-plus years.[87]

In 2006 she found a role with a medium-sized company at the time, Salesforce.

"I felt it was a purpose-driven company and one I wanted to work for. I knew a few people there and was impressed with them," she says, launching a twelve-year career in progressive HR and recruiting roles; today she serves as Salesforce's President and Chief People Officer.

---

87   (Robbins, 2018)

Cindy says, "At the time they were still fairly young, less than one thousand people. And you could feel this energetic culture.

"I actually joined initially as a contractor and had a great manager. I slowly moved up the chain. I worked hard and doors just started to open. Folks brought me up and elevated me."[88]

When asked about her success at the company she shares, "The one thing outside of doing my job effectively that has helped me at Salesforce was learning what my brand wanted to be. And asking what matters for you [the organization]. And for me it was about establishing trusted relationships."

Those relationships gave Cindy not only the support she needed to advance but also grow in herself. "In some cases those relationships led to advocacy and folks in powerful positions being champions of mine. A lot of them helped open the door for me and gave me the edge in becoming comfortable with being uncomfortable."

By 2012, Cindy had risen to Vice President of Executive Search, and 2013 a Vice President of Employee Success, overseeing the Global HR Business Partner program. Cindy describes

---

88 IBD

the transition as, "Moving from a head of recruiting to head of HR was very uncomfortable for me, but I had a mentor who had really pushed me to get outside of my comfort zone."

During her period of growth at the company, the majority of Cindy's support came from men. "Ninety-five percent of my advocates and mentors were men. They held power and influence."

While benefiting from her connection and positive relationships with the leaders of the company, she stayed very close on the imbalances within the organization.

Cindy kept a finger on the pulse of women's issues at Salesforce and the broader market, "I got a lot of feedback in my job in HR about the status of women at the company." This feedback came through formal HR channels and informal feedback from fellow female colleagues.

Cindy evolved into a unique position of overseeing the policies that affected all employees—especially women. She also had the respect and support of senior men.

Asked how she was able to influence the C-Suite to address policies negatively affecting women, she replied, "I have a very good personal friend who is also product executive, Leyla Seeka. We both got promoted into bigger jobs at the same time. It gave us a window to bring items up to Mark [Benioff]."[89]

Mark Benioff is the CEO of Salesforce.

This was 2015 and Cindy had been promoted to Executive Vice President of Global Employee Success, which meant she was the head of global human resources for Salesforce.

"When we went to Mark with a menu of options that we would consider around elevating and retaining women—that included the pay audit—we went to him together. There is power in collaboration and women supporting other women. That was a case of us speaking up. Leyla and I did it together. And there is also no way we could have done that without Mark Benioff."

Mark was in disbelief at first that there was a gap in pay, as he was under the impression that the company was a leader as a place to work. According to an interview with CBS news, Mark's reaction, "It's impossible because we have a great culture here. We're—we're a 'best place to work.'"[90] Through some negotiation Cindy convinced Mark that Salesforce needed to audit their pay.

---

89   IBD
90   (Stahl, 2018)

The results were startling.

To Mark's surprise, "it was throughout the whole company, every division, every department, every geography."[91]

Now a famous event, the company swiftly moved to close the gap in 2015 by giving pay increases to all women whose pay was inappropriately lower than their male counterparts. It cost $3 million in the first year [cite] and the company has remained committed to keeping pay equal.[92]

Cindy describes her experience. "There's not enough women in leadership roles and this is based on statistics. As you rise up the ranks, there's not a lot of us there. So you could feel isolated. I hope other companies will look around the room and say, 'Where are the women?' as Mark did and address it."[93]

UPSHOT

- **Cindy spent the early part of her career getting to know herself and her brand in a variety of roles. This made a difference for her trajectory into more senior roles.**

---

91 IBD
92 IBD
93 (Robbins, 2018)

She became very comfortable learning new things and navigating powerful rooms where she was the "only."

- **Women are in fact helping each other at the top. Even more powerful—their male allies are too.** We're not hearing this story often enough. There is a concerted effort by many men and women at the top to change the status quo.
- **Diversity & Inclusion efforts are making an impact on everyday workers' lives.** Celebrate the quiet champions like Cindy!

* * *

"All things are ready, if our mind be so."

—WILLIAM SHAKESPEARE

Julie Elberfeld
My Approach Is To Change The Narrative.

"I was born in a small Midwest town to hard-working parents," says Julie Elberfeld, SVP of Shared Technology at Capital One and long-time banking Chief Information Officer.[94]

---

94   (Hemmings, 2018)

"As a young girl, I was fascinated with the space program, collecting every article I could find from newspapers and magazines. I even convinced my parents to let me stay home from school once for a launch of one of the Apollo missions—unheard of in our house. I stayed a student of math and science throughout my education and loved learning anything and everything I could."

"My parents fed my thirst and never set any boundaries on what I could become. I majored in Mathematics at Miami University. I started down the path of getting a PhD in Math with a plan for academia but discovered I wasn't cut out for teaching."

"What happened next changed my life. I was invited to learn to be a 'computer programmer' at a bank in Cincinnati. After studying reams of green bar printouts of code, I was soon a self-taught COBOL software engineer."

This solidified Julie's path in engineering and technology in banking.

"My career has been full of new and exciting opportunities, including implementing one of the first home-banking applications in the US in 1995. I was so enthralled with the demanding work of the tech field that my three kids were often found in the office on weekends. My career progressed through various technology leadership roles until I found myself the CIO for Commercial Banking at that same bank."

The bank she is referring to is Fifth Third Bank, where she spent twelve years, before joining Capital One. "In 2009, Capital One recruited me to be their first Commercial Bank CIO, the best move of my career."

Julie's excitement for the application of her passions and ability to transform environments for fellow women is infectious. "We are also completely committed to playing a role in shifting diversity and creating a culture of belonging for all across the technology industry."

"Four years ago, [in 2014] we launched our Women in Tech program internally to elevate our focus on women working in technology. It started when two [female] software engineers in our Technology Development Program came into my office to share their observations from media and college friends that the tech industry was declining in women's representation and some cultures were even hostile to women. These ladies wanted to prevent that from ever interfering with the inclusive culture at Capital One."

"As I contemplated the long-term impacts of the technology industry being devoid of balanced perspectives, combined with how tech is so fundamentally changing the world, I knew something had to be done. I knew the industry that had welcomed me at the start of my career was one many women would love if they could just get to know the possibilities and break through the stereotypes. That meeting turned into a working group, which developed into local chapters that then grew into a movement," says Julie.

Now the movement is in full force.

"The initiative is bringing Capital One women and men together to focus on developing a love of technology in girls, improving the representation of women in the technology field, and supporting the career development of women in tech roles in tangible and impactful ways," she shares.

"Along the way, we've also found meaningful ways to engage with community partners and support their vital work, including Women Who Code, Black Girls Code, Girls Who Code, and AnitaB.org. We have expanded the work to also focus on intersectionality and broader underrepresented groups in Tech, specifically African American and Hispanic people. While we're proud of the work we've done thus far, we're not satisfied. There's more work to do and we're committed to being a part of this journey for as long as it takes."

In a unique role, Julie's responsibilities are split between her tech executive duties and diversity. "I am leading an important and complex portion of our cloud technology journey at Capital One. Not only do I have this interesting technology challenge to tackle, I am also spending 50 percent of my core work on diversity and inclusion in technology at Capital One. I believe it is unique in the industry to have a technology executive focused directly on D&I, supported by, but outside of, Human Resources," says Julie.

Asked about what inspires her to pursue the work, Julie describes, "When I think of the world we will leave for our grandchildren, I know that diversity in the tech field is critical, and it is the right thing to do. Computing jobs are growing three times the average rate of other jobs. Ensuring women and men of color have a welcome seat at the table of technology is my life mission; my approach is to change the narrative."

By changing the narrative, Julie is able to influence not only her work environment but also the inspiration for future generations.

"I've often thought, 'If I were a high school student interested in computer science, but all I saw or read about the field were negative, would I even want to try it?' Or, 'If my children were going to college and considering a tech major, would I encourage them to pursue it or steer them in another direction?'

"Without access to the positive stories of the women and men of color who have stayed in tech and thrived, it's difficult to imagine these children seeing a path for themselves."[95]

Thanks to people like Julie, we can see a path.

UPSHOT

- **Julie's passion for science and technology transcends adversity.** She chooses to share her story of inspiration, which mostly involves a pure love of STEM. The path does not have to be one of struggle.
- **Once in a role of influence, she listened to the trends and challenges facing others and did something about it.** Julie was not ignorant or dismissive of others' experiences that were different than her own.
- **She listened when junior staff approached her and ensured the initiative got its sea legs.** And grew into an organizational movement.

---

95   (Hemmings, 2018)

ACTION ITEMS FOR CAREER DOMINATION

MINDSET

I have the right to trust my employer and colleagues. I cannot control the behaviors of others. I will control own my behavior and redirect my mistrusting mental energy toward creating something of value. There are leaders in positions of power working every day to protect me.

EXERCISE

Prepare yourself to have the ear of someone powerful. No matter who you are, you will run into someone with power and influence at some point—in the elevator, on the sidewalk, waiting in line to buy something, at a conference, at church, etc. Be ready for these moments by:

1. Cultivating conversation starters.
2. Cultivating your curiosities that lead to questions—to keep in the back of your mind.
3. Asking yourself how you could help others by connecting with someone in power.
4. Engaging that person in power on those issues!

Do the listening you wish others were doing. For every moment you feel like you're not being heard—how do you think those around you feel? Likely the same. Notice the times you shut down in a meeting, interview, on the phone, etc. Or better yet, the times you are doing most of the talking. How can you put yourselves in the shoes of others?

CHAPTER 7

TRENCH WARFARE

"In every battle there comes a time when both sides consider themselves beaten. Then he who attacks wins."

—ULYSSES S. GRANT

Conflict. It's uncomfortable. It's hard.

And it's inevitable.

You don't need to man up, but you do need to get ready to fight.

MALADAPTED

When you're me, and you grow up with no healthy guidebook on how to navigate conflict, it can be something you avoid. Okay, let's be honest I really avoid conflict.

When I was a young child, my parents would take their heated arguments behind closed doors in the back of the house. My brother and I could still hear every word of their screaming. Oftentimes the fight would end with someone storming out of the house. There was never any physical violence, but the emotional violence was palpable.

Rarely would we discuss what happened as a family. I never learned how to end an argument healthily or how to do repair work. All I could surmise was that I should prevent fights from ever happening.

My parents divorced when I was ten. Life after the divorce was just as tense and destructive between them. Mostly what changed is that they lived under separate roofs. Through that I learned that resolution is not guaranteed, and love is conditional.

I am not special in my experiences here. A large number of people grow up in unhealthy environments developing maladaptive coping mechanisms before marching in line toward adulthood and joining the workforce.

It's certainly not all of us, but it's enough to cause undue destruction.

The workplace is intended to have little room for our baggage or character flaws. In a perfect capitalist world, we would all compartmentalize our personal from our professional in the exact, robotic way that the Robber barons envisioned for their factories a hundred years ago. Or the modern way corporate executives "see people as 'costs' to be minimized."

What's important is that we acknowledge the fact that this is not a perfect world. People behave badly. We always have options about when or how to address that bad behavior. At work, it is not always our responsibility to handle that behavior, but sometimes it is.

As much as I have wanted to run away from conflict, I've learned that sometimes you need to fight.

* * *

trench warfare

noun

a: warfare in which the opposing forces attack and counterattack from a relatively permanent system of trenches protected by barbed-wire entanglements[96]

* * *

WHY OFFICE LIFE CAN BE A BATTLE

DROPPING A BIAS TRAINING, DIVERSITY INITIA-
TIVE, OR WORK–LIFE PROGRAM INTO WORKPLACES
DOMINATED BY THE MASCULINITY CONTEST DOES
NOT SERVE TO EFFECT MEANINGFUL CHANGE

It is no secret that some work environments in the United States are downright toxic.

A new body of research frames the roots of toxic organizational cultures through what the researchers and authors call "Masculinity Contest Cultures" (MCCs). Dr. Jennifer Berdahl, Dr. Marianne Cooper, Dr. Peter Glick, Dr. Robert Livingston,

---

96 Merriam-Webster, s.v. "trench warfare," accessed June 15, 2019, https://www.merriam-webster.com/dictionary/trench%20warfare

and Joan Williams assembled as an interdisciplinary team to analyze workplaces and the effects of MCCs. Organizations that "foster masculinity contests [do so] by rewarding those who emerge as winners as the 'real men' who are entitled to status and resources."[97]

The researchers present the idea of MCCs as a new way to understand "what goes wrong and why" in organizations like Uber, who the authors highlight as a notorious example (albeit an extreme one).

"Work becomes a masculinity contest when organizations focus not on mission but on masculinity, enacted in endless 'mine's bigger than yours' contests to display workloads and long schedules (as in law and medicine), cut corners to out-earn everyone else, or shoulder unreasonable risks (as in blue-collar jobs or finance)."[98]

To be clear, the researchers define masculinity not by biological gender but rather through social constructs. The authors argue that this gender system is all about power, and people will go to extremes to protect that power.

"In many cultures around the world, males become men through dominance—by controlling other people, 'making

---

97 (Berdahl et al., 2018)
98 IBD

things happen,' eliciting deference, and resisting being controlled by others."

Here's how that plays out. "Organizations with MCCs valorize hegemonic masculinity, or the traits men 'ought' to have—being aggressive, assertive, independent, ambitious, competitive, and strong—and disparage femininity, or the traits men 'ought not' have—sensitivity, naiveté, weakness, insecurity, gullibility, uncertainty, and indecisiveness."

"Much of our own work has exposed how masculine pressures on men motivate them to engage in 'bad but bold' behavior—including sexual harassment, physical aggression, extreme work hours and cut-throat competition."

The authors further explain. "The masculinity contest concept focuses on how the very acts that serve to signify an individual man's masculinity can come to define an organization's culture. In this zero-sum game, men compete at work for dominance by showing no weakness, demonstrating a single-minded focus on professional success, displaying physical endurance and strength, and engaging in cut-throat competition. We characterize a company as having an MCC when these behaviors are not just the isolated acts of a few individual men but become the way work gets done; i.e., when masculine norms determine who and what gets rewarded, how colleagues should be treated, and attitudes about work/life balance."

Given this entrenched culture, the authors explain why D&I initiatives are not effective. "Dropping a bias training, diversity initiative, or work–life program into workplaces dominated by the masculinity contest does not serve to effect meaningful change."

From this research, one can surmise that you go to battle when you are trapped in a masculinity contest. You can either win the contest or fight to eliminate it. As the authors describe, "Eliminating the masculinity contest will help organizations focus on efficiency and profitability rather than on macho showmanship and will help all workers who want to be left in peace to do their work with dignity."[99]

* * *

"You may have to fight a battle more than once to win it."

—MARGARET THATCHER

---

99   (Berdahl et al., 2018)

THIS IS WHAT A BATTLEFIELD LOOKS LIKE

In 2012, Ellen Pao sued one of the most powerful and influential Venture Capital firms in the United States, Kleiner Perkins Caufield & Byers (KPCB), which was her employer, for gender discrimination. She knew her odds of winning the case in court were not in her favor, but she did it anyway.

Ellen joined KPCB in 2005 as chief of staff to John Doerr, Chairman. This was a highly competitive and prestigious position. The job requirements were lengthy, quirky, and a perfect match for her rare background in law, business, and engineering. She described the role as "thrilling" and also saw signs from the beginning that the environment would not be as supportive of women in the same ways as men. "Sometimes the whole world felt like a nerdy frat house," said Ellen about venture capital (VC) life in Silicon Valley.[100]

In her time at KPCB she observed everything from micro-aggressions to serious impediments in advancing careers. "At VC meetings, male partners frequently spoke over female colleagues or repeated what the women said and took the credit. Women were admonished when they 'raised their voices' yet chastised when they couldn't 'own the room.' In that round of summer reviews [in 2011], Kleiner had six junior partners who had worked there for four or more years. The women

---

100 (Pao et al., 2017)

had twice as many years at Kleiner, but only the men got promoted."[101]

Other examples involved male leaders excluding women from events where key business discussions took place. Ellen describes, "At one point I found out the partners had taken some CEOs and founders on an all-male ski trip. They spent fifty thousand dollars on the private jet to and from Vail. I was later told that they didn't invite any women because women probably wouldn't want to share a condo with men."

Making the situation more complex, Ellen had a brief affair, what she called, "a short-lived, sporadic fling" with her colleague—under the impression he was separated from his wife. To her shock, she later discovered he was still married and had lied to her. Ellen ended the relationship immediately.

Over time, her former lover and colleague retaliated by growing hostile and excluding Ellen from information and important meetings, eventually influencing her performance reviews in damaging ways. "Not only was he blocking my work, he had been promoted to a position of even greater responsibility and was giving me negative reviews."

---

101 IBD

When John Doerr hired Ellen initially, he pitched her on KPCB's desire to hire women into senior roles and its status as one of the only VC firms in Silicon Valley to do so. When asked by an investigator later in her tenure why the firm had hired women, if only to block or ignore them, Ellen said, "If you had the opportunity to have workers who were overeducated, underpaid, and highly experienced, whom you could dump all the menial tasks you didn't want to do on, whom you could get to clean up all the problems, and whom you could create a second class out of, wouldn't you want them to stay?"[102]

* * *

LAUNCHING A BATTLE CAMPAIGN

The official claim Ellen filed in her case, "specified gender discrimination in promotion and pay, and retaliation against me after I reported the harassment." Because of her job title, economic advantages, and leadership as a woman to sue KPCB, Ellen's case became high profile and covered by the national media. Her and her husband's lives became fodder for gossip and conjecture and she reported eventually their "privacy destroyed."

---

102 (Pao et al., 2017)

Ellen knew in advance this would happen, having investigated her options thoroughly. "Before suing, I'd consulted other women who had sued big, powerful companies over harassment and discrimination, and they all gave me pretty much the same advice: 'Don't do it'... One woman told me, 'It's a complete mismatch of resources. They don't fight fair. Even if you win, it will destroy your reputation.'"

So why did Ellen decide to fight the brutal court battle, including national attention? In her words, "I'll grant that only someone a little bit masochistic would sign up for the onslaught of personal attacks that comes with a high-profile case... I was one of the only people who had the resources and the position to do so. I believed I had an obligation to speak out about what I'd seen."[103]

* * *

"If you think you are too small to make a difference, try sleeping with a mosquito."

—THE DALAI LAMA

---

103 IBD

THE PAO-WER OF ONE WOMAN

Ellen's grit, tenacity, and strong moral compass in the midst of a brutal fight while at KPCB and afterward defined her character and paved the way for a new path for herself and a new movement of women to quickly stand up to entrenched discrimination in the tech industry.

According to Jessi Hempel of *Wired*, "There were so many times Ellen Pao could have taken money in exchange for silence. Before she filed her gender discrimination lawsuit... she could have negotiated a severance, preserving relationships. She did not. At three intervals after she filed suit, Kleiner attempted to settle, offering her significant money (at one point she reported that the figure was likely between three and five million) in exchange for her silence. Pao pursued a trial... Even after that, she said she turned down a $2.7 million payment from Kleiner that would have covered her legal costs because the firm requested that she sign a non-disparagement clause. That could have at least recouped her legal fees, and those that Kleiner demanded she cover. By then, many of the firm's worst offenses had been aired publicly, and we all would have understood if Pao had chosen to take the money and repair to Hawaii."[104]

---

104 (Hempel, 2018)

Hempel continues, "But the point of Pao's suit was never the money. Pao refused to sign the gag order, and instead recorded her story in a memoir entitled *Reset: My Fight for Inclusion and Lasting Change*. Pao used the book to reveal, at long last, what she was thinking and how she was feeling in the run-up to her trial and as she forged a new career path as a very public figure."[105]

A self-described introvert, and someone who shies away from the limelight, Pao's emergence as a national, visible leader seems surprising and also authentic. She describes her journey. "More personally, I've come out of the experience with great friends and supporters. We've changed jobs, started companies, taken time off, moved across the country, and switched careers. I've watched as each of us—myself included—has become more vocal, more open, and more courageous in advocating for change in tech."[106]

In choosing to go public and fight for what she felt was right, Ellen transformed herself from a venture capitalist to a change agent.

The impact of her decisions and actions has had a ripple effect. Hempel writes, "Many women have spoken up this year, demanding fair treatment across the tech industry.

---

105 IBD
106 (Pao et al., 2017)

They're less afraid of retribution than they once were, and they're more certain of the strength of their own voices to force a public reckoning in Silicon Valley. Among tech circles, there's a name for this. It's The Pao Effect."[107]

UPSHOT

- **All the signs in Ellen's environment pointed to a war zone.** She was surrounded by behavior of aggression, violence, discrimination, and that unfitting of a professional workplace. Egregious. These are the signs that one must take action.

- **Women are qualified, have the desire, and get in the game even in toxic organizations.** Ellen was stimulated and eager to work in a fast-pace and demanding environment. The macho culture caught her off guard and yet she stuck with it anyway; they did not chase her off. The narrative that women cannot handle this is moot.

- **Even though Ellen did not win the case, she made a tremendous impact on the public's awareness and perception of Silicon Valley workplaces.** People like Ellen who have wealth, clout, and know-how are fighting for the rest of us daily. She could have walked away with the rewards but instead chose to fight on our behalf.

---

107 (Hempel, 2018)

- **Becoming a warrior ended positively for Ellen.** She found a new career, maintained her integrity, and gained respect nationally for her efforts, despite the gossip and public shaming.
- **We can call her General Pao.** By taking such bold risks, she inspired other women to become lieutenants and follow her lead.

ACTION ITEMS FOR CAREER DOMINATION

MINDSET

I am a warrior. I have the strength to withstand whatever they throw at me. I work to provide for myself, my family, and my overall livelihood because it matters. No one has the right to sully my productivity with inexcusable behavior. That will not stand.

EXERCISE

Play defense. Starting with defense is not a sign of weakness. In many situations it can be the best offense. Stay neutral in tense situations. Rally an emotional support system from your community of friends, family, and colleagues not associated with the situation. Maintain physical and emotional distance from bad actors. Change departments, offices, or teams. Get out of firing range.

Get your weapons. Document. Report all behavior to your superiors or leaders in the organization. Consult your mentors and sponsors from the outset. Better yet, consult with people external from your organization. Keep up your armor; do your job. Network externally and internally regarding other job opportunities or projects; amass exit options. Forge relationships with other warriors. Enlist your support system for the long-haul.

Make a strategy. No situation is alike and you always have options. Leverage your key allies, weapons, and best defense as a total formula. Most importantly, wait to engage until your strategy is clear, rational, and one that can minimize risks to the level you can handle.

PART 4

EXPAND

[amplify; extend; boost; accelerate; unfurl; proliferate]

To perform at a high level, you'll need to pick up speed. Take yourself to new levels and shamelessly influence.

Get in the game!

CHAPTER 8

DISRUPTION

———

"Everybody has a plan until they get punched in the face."

—MIKE TYSON

What will you do when things fall apart?

Because they will.

EVACUATE

Quitting was brilliant. I needed to quit; I had to quit. All I could think about for weeks was quitting if not months or really almost a year—and I was scared shitless.

It was early 2018 and I was the bread-winning lesbian mom whose wife had given birth to a baby with no intention of going back to work. It was all on me.

Our immediate savings had gone to our new parenting life and my one investment account I was so proud of building was all that stood between us and destitution if I quit my job. (Let's not talk about those untouchable retirement accounts and when you start investigating how to drain them decades early.)

I felt the fear of failure like a hellish hot anvil pressing on my chest. Sometimes it would well up and come over me in random and very safe places—like the grocery store or at a potluck.

My situation at work had been complex for quite a while.

My early performance reviews had painted me as a rising star. In the beginning, I had a supportive boss and she later gave me the risky, yet high profile projects no one else had wanted—and rewarded me when I executed them.

Yet those projects took their toll with long hours, ambiguity, and not a lot of support. Throw in a grueling culture of high performance, my new baby life, and some genuine mistakes that reflected poorly on my manager, and I had a recipe for eventual burnout.

The tipping point came on a hot June day when I missed a key detail on one of my most important projects that influenced a large negotiation. I owned it, but my boss refused to defend me to upper management. Someone senior called me and rained down the heat on my performance hardcore. It was so intimidating that I proceeded to have the first panic attack in my life.

In the office.

Holy shit they're going to fire me for this and it was so avoidable.

I called my wife and I called my most trusted work friend; both counseled me through it. I went home and tried to find some sanity. There were tears and Oh My God What the Fuck Am I Going To Do.

When I returned to work the next day and coming weeks, no one mentioned the events again. I was quietly removed from the last parts of the project. Instead of an outward reprimand, my tasks on that project went away.

It was eerie—I was shaken—and clear I still had a job.

This is the point at which I would have coached someone else to thank their lucky stars, regroup, and start kicking ass at the job again. Everyone has their low points; everyone makes mistakes. Heck employees go through much worse every day all across the world, and here were my employers actually keeping me around (at least in the short term).

But I chose something different.

Three weeks later I resigned with no offers in hand. I had a wife, a baby, a threadbare exit strategy on our apartment, and a phone call to our closest family to say, "Fuck this. We're moving back home."

That was the first time I saw firsthand how toxic workplaces make diversity matters moot. Tough shit can happen to anyone in a bad environment.

And I got the hell out.

* * *

risk

/ risk /

verb

1: to expose to hazard or danger
2: to incur the risk or danger of[108]

Science tells us that we are all influenced in our upbringing by the outcomes of the risks we take.[109] Those whose risks pay off develop stronger risk-taking muscles over time. While those who experienced the pain of more frequent failed risks can grow more risk-averse.

Risk is a tough topic to navigate when you're less privileged or leveraged in your life. The stakes are higher for exposing yourself when you have fewer safety nets than those with more wealth, power, and structural support.

You could say I'm mostly risk averse. I've made a lot of safe choices in my career, and smartly (although mostly unintentionally) invested in building up a safety net. In my family,

---

108 Merriam-Webster, s.v. "risk," accessed June 15, 2019, https://www. merriam-webster.com/dictionary/risk
109 (Brooks, 2016)

I am the physical safety net for everyone else. Thus, I have trained myself to embody stability at all levels.

It gets really nuanced when you learn you can embody stability while also taking risks—like quitting a job with seemingly no backup plan. And in fact, if I am going to take my career to new levels and heights I'm going to have to learn even more about risk-taking.

Simply put, while risk-aversion may seem to be a smart strategy, it can get in the way of success.

"Everyone wants to be more successful, even though definitions of success vary wildly... there's one pattern of thinking that's important to achieving any measure of success, no matter how you define it... being comfortable taking risks," says Sam McRoberts, Philosopher and CEO of Vudu Media.[110]

Here are the lessons I drew from quitting my job:

1) Learn the difference between fear and gut instinct

As Author Amy Morin writes: "When it comes to taking risks, there's something to be said for trusting your gut. But too many people confuse a gut instinct with fear. They assume

---

110 (McRoberts, 2017)

their discomfort means their gut is telling them not to proceed. So rather than step outside their comfort zone, they avoid the risks that could propel them forward. Whether they stay stuck in a job they don't like or pass up a new business opportunity, many people struggle to calculate risk. They assume if something feels scary, it must be really risky. But that's not an accurate way to measure risk."[111]

2) Learn to calculate risk

Consciously calculating risk is a tangible skill. There is a common belief that successful people have no fear and dive head-first into risky situations, which in turn leads to breakthroughs and wins.

The reality is that very successful people take the risks they have first deliberated extensively and then have found ways to minimize the risk overall. The bets they take are not random.

As Richard Branson says, "Superficially, I think it looks like entrepreneurs have a high tolerance for risk. But one of the most important phrases in my life is 'protect the downside.'"

---

111 (Morin, 2017)

In a business world where the idea of "disruption" has become sexy, we might pause to consider the reality of what's happening behind the marketing campaign.

Disruption has consequences, whether or not you asked or planned for them. Better to make a plan.

* * *

"Geniuses are always marginalized to one degree or another. Someone wholly invested in the status quo is unlikely to disrupt it."

—ERIC WEINER

Candice Matthews Brackeen
I'm just a starter. I start things.

"I think I've always had an adventurous spirit, but not necessarily the entrepreneurial spirit," says Candice Matthews Brackeen, Co-founder and Executive Director of Cincinnati start-up accelerator, Hillman Accelerator.[112]

---

112 (Merritt, 2018)

Candice grew up in the Midwest as the only girl in a modest home.

"I have five brothers. I come from a pretty humble upbringing. My dad is an electrician; my mom works in a local regional bank. I just wanted to be out and do things and experience things. Maybe that hunger from having a humble upbringing forced me into figuring out how I would be able to experience more things."

Driven, she studied Economics at the University of Cincinnati, graduating in 2004, and started working in strategy consulting. With the later birth of her two sons just two years apart—she soon chose to stay at home full time.

Along the way she became a personal trainer and decided to own her own business as a way to re-enter the workforce.

In 2010, Candice launched her first business, a brick-and-mortar wellness studio called The Body Boutique. This turned into a mom and baby fitness company called Fit Mommies and eventually, in 2014 she founded a digital service called Hello Parent.

Along the Hello Parent journey, she became involved with an Ohio technology accelerator called UpTech, which offered education, mentoring, and access to networks and capital.

Hello Parent started out as a blog and evolved into a full-blown application designed specifically for parents.

Unfortunately, Hello Parent did not survive.

"We were named [by Cincinnati reporters] 'The Greatest Failure and Lesson Learned.' I learned how to raise money. I learned how to lose money. And I learned from all those mistakes. It was really a glorious failure," says Candice.[113]

THE STATE OF BLACK FEMALE ENTREPRENEURSHIP

The number of firms owned by black women in the US grew by an exciting 164 percent from 2007 to 2018.[114]

In that same time period, women-owned businesses grew just 58 percent.

As of 2018, there are 2.4 million black-women-owned businesses. These are big numbers. Why?

"It's pretty evident that one of the primary reasons for black women to start businesses is frustrations on the job," says

---

113 (Merritt, 2018)
114 (Hannon, 2018)

Dell Gines, who authored a report on the matter for the Federal Reserve Bank of Kansas.[115]

"They feel they can't get anywhere...There's a feeling of being passed over for promotions, a sense of workplace fatigue, of being asked to train people to be their boss."

Unfortunately, the size of their businesses tend to be micro. "The businesses tend to stay very small, and you don't see a lot of scalability," he says.

"On average, annual sales at businesses owned by black women are two times smaller than the next-lowest demographic group, Hispanic women, and close to five times smaller than for all women-owned businesses, according to the Federal Reserve. The average annual sales for businesses owned by black women was $27,752 in 2012 (the most recent figures available), compared to $143,731 for all women and $170,587 for white women," says Gines.

According to the Federal Reserve report, one reason so many of the businesses are small is that many black women have difficulty accessing credit and face capital constraints.

But there are people working to change that.

------

115 IBD

The report had a positive outlook, according to Gines. "You are going to see a rise in black women doing business in professional services with the rapid increase in education levels for black women and their increased participation in the labor market, in fields such as accounting and engineering."[116]

Slowly but surely.

Candice Matthews parted ways with Hello Parent in late 2016 with the idea for a new accelerator—one focused on minority founders—in the works.

"This is the seventh thing I've started," says Candice regarding the Hillman Accelerator. In early 2017, she partnered with former Cincinnati Bengal and current (private equity firm) Qey Capital chairman Dhani Jones and Ebow Vroom also of Qey Capital to launch.[117]

"I founded the Black Founders Network back in June of 2015. We were meeting monthly with a group of eleven. Over the last three years, we raised, like, $45 million as a group—just with our separate companies. We started to notice that the group was robust and winning with the network we already had. Dhani invited the group to his house to talk about how we can expand, and from that conversation came the

116 (Hannon, 2018)
117 (Merritt, 2018)

Hillman Accelerator. It's a way for black founders to get into the accelerators here in Cincinnati," says Candice.

The Hillman Accelerator is the first in the Midwest to provide support specifically to tech companies with founders from underserved communities. The name was inspired by the TV show, "A Different World." The popular "Cosby" spin-off took place at the fictional, predominantly black Hillman College.

"Letting people see that it's normalizing the winds for women and minorities in tech and innovation. It's letting people see that you can have success. It's letting people understand that this is not a risky business. This isn't even a niche. This is America. We are educated. I want people to see that we're working hard," says Candice.[118]

Indeed they are. The accelerator is now one of the largest women and minority-led in the country.

UPSHOT

- **Creating something new takes countless tries.** Once you commit to your creation, spend time preparing yourself for all the attempts you'll need to get there.

---

118 (Hannon, 2018)

- **Early failures aren't always failures. Sometimes just unfinished versions of future creations.** The process is iterative!
- **Candice incorporated her personal intersections distinctly into her business ideas.** Her own unique qualities helped her businesses stand out and grow.

* * *

"Courage does not always roar. Sometimes it is the quiet voice at the end of the day saying, 'I will try again tomorrow.'"

—MARY ANN RADMACHER

Laura Welch
Ideally There's Someone With More Lived Experiences Who Can Show You What's Possible.

"Diversity is a key question for candidates looking at top companies and organizations. We're seeing this especially in our surveys of young talent on campus who are coming to Citi. Diversity is one of the main reasons they are attracted to us, or our globality," says Laura Welch, former Vice-President and Talent & Diversity Manager for Citi.

"I've worked in this space for some time. Originally I was attracted to Diversity & Inclusion because I knew what it felt like (as a woman and person of color especially) not to have examples of people who looked like me in the spaces I inhabited. Ideally there's someone with more lived experiences who can show you what's possible."

Laura started her career as a banking analyst in 2008 with Citi before transitioning to human capital consulting with Deloitte in 2010 and finally returning to Citi to launch a progression of Diversity & Inclusion (D&I) and human resources roles in 2014 (after a two-year full-time MBA program at Tuck School of Business at Dartmouth). She currently works at Flatiron Health where she manages their leadership development and talent management efforts.

She fully embraced her D&I focus at Citi, fueled by the desire to influence policies and the structural barriers diverse employees face. "Work [can be] one of the only places where you're exposed to people from a wide range of backgrounds and experiences. We tend to be homogeneous in our home lives and communities. But coming to work can force you to interact with people different from you," she says.

Fast forward four years to 2018 and Laura is feeling the fatigue of her Diversity & Inclusion work, a common occurrence in the practitioner community.

"Being a Black D&I practitioner working on the strategy for black and brown employees can grow tiring after a while. At Citi, we have found that when those with more institutional power, namely, cis-gender white men, step up and champion diversity initiatives, it can help accelerate progress. I hope to see a more diverse cross-section of leaders championing diversity and inclusion initiatives in the future but know that will be a long road."

Change is slow. It's a marathon.

"What I've seen over time is that the way you change representation is not solely through events, ERG's or councils but through looking at the processes that allow employees to get identified, promoted and paid."

So what happens to someone like Laura feeling the fatigue in their role? Oftentimes, women in her shoes leave to start their own companies.

As Laura describes, "Some of the highest rates of entrepreneurship are among women of color. This is a generalization, but oftentimes, women of color tend to possess key traits, such as grit and resilience, that make them particularly talented entrepreneurs. Laura sees two ways for her to have an impact with her D&I and talent expertise - advising women and people of color on the corporate track and entrepreneurial track on how to navigate the systems in which they operate."

Laura sees two ways for her to make an impact with her deep Diversity & Inclusion experience: advising entrepreneurs or advising women and people of color on navigating corporate structures. "But the problem of being different within corporate structures is always having to flex who you are," and thus the power and appeal of entrepreneurship.

"Many black women say, 'I'm going to hold on and they'll do right by me' within their companies but it never happens."

Starting a business is a big deal. "There are incredible resources out there for all entrepreneurs, not just for women and people of color. It really can empower women to take the leap," says Laura.

"The challenge so many women and people of color face is scaling their companies and securing proper funding." Once your business reaches a certain stage, you need outside capital to scale and this is where women and people of color have a huge disadvantage."

Just as the barriers that exist within large companies, those same prejudices and limits exist in the Venture Capital and financing communities—as we've seen.

Lucky for us, Laura keeps working, coaching, and guiding organizations, colleagues, and entrepreneurs alike.

UPSHOT

- **Amazing and accomplished people feel burnout too.** In the face of this, they find a way to continue making an impact.
- **Know yourself and what depletion looks like.** Laura regularly checks in with herself and identifies where she is feeling energy loss. Shedding light on this empowers you to address it.

ACTION ITEMS FOR CAREER DOMINATION

MINDSET

I am a brave son of a bitch. That's right you are. It may be crass, you may cringe, and it's totally true. For every decision you have made that got you this far, acknowledge that deep inside you have the strength to tackle any professional challenge you'll ever encounter. Repeat this mantra, and don't back down from the impossible.

Hire a coach. To prevent burnout or before making a major change in your career, you need an unbiased party. You need an engaged mirror (person) to help you see yourself and to help you see and balance the logic and emotions of your decisions. Of your many resources for advice—family, friends, mentors, colleagues—none can meet the sweet spot of sophistication-experience-ability to see you as clearly as a coach. And because you are paying the coach, their bias is much less than someone who loves you.

Hire a good coach. Okay so everyone and their brother these days is a "life coach" or a "career coach" or an "executive coach." Finding a good one in the midst of all the noise (I mean, how can you even benchmark what's good?) is quite the challenge. There are countless online resources with guides on how to find someone. Invest the time to understand what is healthy to expect from a coach and what you are looking to get from the relationship.

CHAPTER 9

TEMPERED STEEL

———

"Currents of air and sea are vulnerable to my breathing. Metaphors of mountain ranges seem tiny compared to all I contain."

—LAURIE PEREZ

You cannot be contained.

GETTING OUT

The first time I heard author, actor, and producer, Jacob Tobia, speak in person was at a conference in New York City for queer women.

Jacob was standing on stage with the longest legs, truly high heels, and a full beard. They (Jacob goes by the pronoun "they") gave a talk on gender that I never fathomed. It was edgy, sleek, and palatable. It had all the elements I had intuited about gender and could never quite put my finger on or spell out—the fluidity, the societal pressures and norms, and Jacob's raw story of coming out as gender-queer.

Seeing Jacob stand there so confidently poised (and much better dressed than any of us) with a snazzy Prezi visual presentation, which succinctly deconstructed modern gender, I felt insecure immediately. I had never seen someone embody and own—what Jacob calls—"all the genders." Both masculine and feminine fully expressed in one person with grace, strength, and professionalism.

I was looking at the future.

Every time I've ever interviewed for a job I've thought hard about what to wear. It wasn't just "which outfit fits the company," it was more "what if they can tell I'm gay from the outset?" and "will they judge me before they know me?" The thought naturally continues into what to wear at work every day, and how one presents oneself for career success in general.

Watching Jacob speak, I could see in their appearance that they were out in front of all of us with their personal brand and knew what we thought. Jacob was five steps ahead and had cultivated how they would be perceived and loved/owned/embraced it.

Jacob's personal presentation was like the summary of long-tested and developed personal identity thesis. I had to ask:

How do the rest of us get there?

Jacob had a calling.

* * *

ikigai

YOUR REASON TO GET UP IN THE MORNING.

The Japanese concept of ikigai has gained popularity around the world in recent years. Many cite *National Geographic* reporter Dan Buettner's 2009 TED talk, "How to Live to be 100+," as the linchpin for ikigai's global spread. In the talk, Buettner attributes ikigai as a reason for the Japanese citizens' long lives, especially for those on the island of Okinawa where ikigai is considered a way of life.[119]

---

119 (Buettner, 2009)

Renowned Japanese Neuroscientist Ken Mogi describes the concept, "In Japanese, *iki* means 'to live' and *gai* means 'reason'—in other words, your reason to live."[120]

Where the concept appears radical to the West is in its view of retirement. In his TED talk, Buettner describes it this way:

In America, we divide our adult life into two categories: Our work life and our retirement life. In Okinawa, there isn't even a word for retirement. Instead there's simply 'ikigai,' which essentially means 'the reason for which you wake up in the morning.'[121]

This is the idea that one never needs to retire from the thing one was born to do. So you'll see one-hundred-plus-year-old Okinawans doing the work they've always done—even in their latest years—with meaning.

* * *

"Purpose, it's that little flame that lights a fire under your ass."

—AVENUE Q

---

120 (Mogi, 2019)
121 (Buettner, 2009)

Jacob Tobia
When I Think About My Career, I Can't Decide What's Been More Disruptive For It—my Gender Identity Or Being An Artist.

Jacob grew up in North Carolina in the late 1990s and early 2000s and their first major foray into establishing an adult identity was navigating their gender and sexual identities. "For the last decade of my life, in terms of how I thought about myself, my identity developed first as a gay teen and by age eighteen more as gender nonconforming, and then as queer and trans-identity."

A high performer, Jacob was somehow able to navigate the experience while maintaining high academic achievements and was accepted to Duke University for undergraduate studies in 2010.

They noticed in both high school and college the pressure to conform in their future jobs and career. "I went to a college preparatory high school and Duke undergrad where the idea of being an artist feels foolish, like the idea of graduating and taking a job that doesn't give you a 401K is failing."

Jacob battled dual pressures: to fit in with the prescribed social norms of career paths as well as to tone down their queerness. "I felt the pressure to be a model queer. If I was going to be the token kid in heels, I needed to be really good at the stand-up path."

To navigate the complexities of Jacob's evolving young identity and pressures to conform to a prescribed mold, they made key decisions about where to focus their energies. "What was front burner when I was younger was the idea of trying to make the world more and more navigable for people like me—and the idea of what I want to do as a person in this world was back burner... The thing that felt safe, that appealed to my performative and storytelling sensibilities, felt more like the political route."

Thus, Jacob pursued a bachelor of arts in Human Rights Advocacy and Leadership at Duke, with the thought of moving to Washington, DC after graduation in 2014.

"I moved to [Washington], DC and was immediately miserable. It's a really hard thing to be a gender nonconforming person in DC. You feel you're an 'other' always."

As Jacob had followed the conventional wisdom to move for opportunities in government and the [LGBT] political movement, they also realized, "The LGBT movement really had no place for me and the way I wanted to be artistically." In a very "un-Duke student-like thing to do," Jacob picked up and moved to Manhattan after only three months with no job prospects or network. "I took the first office job I could find and was there for nine months. The environment was better, and yet the job wasn't what I wanted to be doing long term."

The atmosphere of New York was much more interesting and a better fit than DC and Jacob immersed themselves in meeting new people who interested them—gravitating to those in media, entertainment, and the arts.

Jacob dabbled in freelance work until in 2015 and found a new day job with the Astrea Lesbian Foundation, which was much more organizational, logistical and an environment, "Where I felt fully supported and seen and validated." For the first time, Jacob left work feeling energized and able and eager to pursue writing on the side—their true passion. The city, the job, and freedom inspired a feverish output of side projects and activity. "I started Instagramming my face off, which led to a web series I created for NBC News and networking in earnest about a career in the entertainment industry, specifically the TV-side of things."

The hustle paid off.

"I was able to build some wonderful relationships within the trans community involved with the show 'Transparent,' which led to me flying out to California to meet with the writers group. Three months later I had a job offer to move there and work on the show," says Jacob.

The opportunity was a springboard and also the linchpin to Jacob's current work in acting, producing, and writing—with articles in major publications such as *The New York Times*, *Washington Post, Time, Teen Vogue, Playboy*, and many others. Jacob also has two major television projects in production and a newly published, best-selling memoir called *Sissy*.

Noticeable in Jacob's experience is how critical visibility is to their career success. Jacob works in industries where you have to be *seen* to remain relevant. Entertainment audiences are notoriously brutal bullshit sniffers. A lesser person would have melted under the scrutiny.

It's a good thing Jacob did all that work on themselves first.

UPSHOT

- **Stay fresh on "know thyself."** Jacob pays attention and responds when they encounter pain. When a city isn't supportive, they move. When a job isn't a good fit, they find a new one. When their network isn't evolved, they reach out to new people. And yet these were not empty decisions—rather calculated in preventing situations (and their internal landscape) from festering.

- **Keep moving**. All that relocating and action serves Jacob by flapping their wings (like a duck releasing energy after a fight) at every juncture in their evolving identity and skill sets.
- **That little voice in your head is your moneymaker.** The voice may say weird or unusual things and that's good. Listen to it.

DIAMONDS ARE FOREVER

When I began writing this book, I thought it would be about transformation. I feel so transformed as an individual; the word resonates with me. Cue visual of butterfly emerging from the cocoon.

And then I realized that transformation means that the thing undergoing transformation must change completely in form, and thus it was flawed or doomed from the start. There is an important distinction between being doomed from the start and enhancing the underlying beauty of a thing.

I had the wrong thought. I have not changed in form. Rather I have responded to adversity by getting bigger, by growing.

It's the same way diamonds form inside the Earth's crust. Diamonds are carbon atoms forced together through high temperatures and insane pressure. This happens one hundred miles below the Earth's surface where the force and heat are so tremendous—and the environment so brutal and unforgiving—that gorgeous crystals grow and emerge.

Somehow in the midst of compact space, the carbon atoms expand. Like, how do they *blossom* in a pressure cooker? How do they emerge *refined?*

As violent and brutal as it sounds, the process is sophisticated, nuanced, and beautiful.

And those diamonds last forever.

* * *

"Understanding your own story is a powerful way to think about the future."

—G. RICHARD SHELL

George Walker
No one deserves the privilege of being themselves any more than I do.

"I came out [of the Peace Corps] more black, more gay, and more Christian," says George Walker after his experience in Ecuador with the Peace Corps in the mid-1990s.

Today he is an influential, national Diversity & Inclusion leader and he references his time in Ecuador as pivotal to his career.

"You start with this knowledge that you're going to help people. What happens to most volunteers is they get there and realize they end up getting more done *for* them than actually doing for other people. Part of it is going through this process of learning the distinction between useful and helpful."

George realized swiftly how to navigate the experience.

"Every Peace Corps volunteer has a different experience and my focus was on youth development. We were in a very marginalized, very poor part of Guayaquil, one of the largest cities in Ecuador. We adapted an education program to teach them about drugs, HIV, and self-esteem. I had a coworker, who we called "counterpart"; mine was incredible. It ensured that we were teaching people to fish instead of just giving them fish."

Working in a new environment with strong, self-confident peers affected George.

"In terms of my own self-awareness, I was not immediately out when I went to the Peace Corps. But my roommate was out as a proud gay man even though there were safety concerns we all had to consider," says George.

"His inspiration pushed me because I thought, 'He doesn't deserve the privilege of being himself any more than I do.' And that was clear. I was very proud [already] of being African American and who my family was. We had a really proud community. We didn't feel like blackness made us second seat to anybody.

"I started to feel liberated there, but it was definitely clear when I came back to the US. Often black is in juxtaposition to whiteness and whiteness doesn't get talked about.

"It was very different being Ecuador. People didn't think about my race. It was the first place where I was really seen as an American. It wasn't always good but that's what you were. You had money, status, something else. You were a Gringo irrespective of your race. That was something I wasn't as used to.

"This shaped how I ended up in Diversity & Inclusion work. D&I was never a job I knew I could do. There is some irony because I did know Roosevelt Thomas (one of the founding leaders of D&I) as a member of my church and his business partner Thurmond Woodard. Both had huge impacts on D&I. I saw it but didn't know that's ultimately what I would be doing."

His time in Ecuador and with the Peace Corps taught George how to integrate his identity and skills to inspire a future career in diversity work.

"When I came back from Peace Corps, I was just more inter-sectional in my approach. That way of walking really came to shape what I wanted to do.

"I think most people who do this work do it from a space that is beyond their control. If you look at an athlete, like a Pete Sampras, Billy Jean King, etc.—someone who has given their all to their sport. There were plenty of times along the way when they would have burned out. Yet there was something inside them that constantly said, 'This is the thing that keeps you going.'

"Some people do burn out, whether in athletics or music. Maybe they were in it for the wrong things and they burned out. I think when you really care about what you're doing... when you have a model of something that's bigger than yourself, you will continue until you can't anymore."

When you meet George today, you'll find a thoughtful, energized person fully confident in who they are personally and professionally.

He continues.

UPSHOT

- **Service work can help you get out of your own way**. There are countless stories of transformative Peace Corps experiences, and they will continue to be powerful for this very reason.
- **George was deeply curious about all parts of his identity.** You are a dynamic human being with intersections of passions, interests, and experiences. Get curious about those intersections. George's distinction was more than just one aspect of himself. It was the combination of multiple.
- **George expanded the pride he felt in one part of his identity to others**. A natural extension.

ACTION ITEMS FOR CAREER DOMINATION

MINDSET

There is a higher purpose here, and I will come from a place of service. Both Jacob and George embodied a service mindset in a way that launched their careers. Even if they did not know where they were going, they knew where to start—by putting themselves in other people's shoes. Those environments became the mirrors in which they could see themselves better. The practice of thinking about how you can help or offer value translates to all future career paths, discussions, and roles.

EXERCISE

Be clear about who you are and what you bring to the table to craft your elevator pitch. You'll need this story for every network contact. People cannot help you if you are not clear about who you are, what you offer, the skills you have, and your motivation. If you're a PR guy, be the PR guy. If you're an artist, be the artist. Seasoned and influential people (recruiters, hiring managers, your future colleagues, people who have the power to help you) can tell by your résumé, LinkedIn, and in-person presence who you are/what you offer even if you can't. Those who come to the conversation about themselves with their own elevator pitch hashed out and clear move faster through the process.

Look in the mirror and chant, *"I'm hot as fuck."* Jacob Tobia recommends this as a regular ritual. They instructed me to tell people on the street, customer service staff in venues, friends, family, enemies, everyone. It's like an energy bar for yourself.

PARTING THOUGHTS

I am optimistic. Forever and always, optimistic.

Those of us who are different have more visibility than we've ever had. The empathy we receive publicly and behind closed doors is real. People care, as do those in power. While we are disappointed in the status quo, it does not negate the gains we *have* made over the decades. The demographics of the US population are changing in noticeable ways. The change is pressuring the old guard of white power norms and systems, and while some are lashing back, others are growing and receptive. The voices fighting for us are getting stronger and louder.

We're on a path toward greater acceptance of workplace Otherness. The definition of "Other" is broad and strikes a chord even with those who don't seem "other" on the surface. Our numbers are growing.

This is a call for you, my diverse careerists, to bring your best (and sometimes most contrary!) qualities to the table. We want you—your grit, resilience, vibrancy, creativity, enthusiasm, and intuition.

Companies need the distinctive warriors, the Hurricane Force Women, and the diamonds in the rough. Employers know they cannot predict the work or customer bases of the future, but they have a sense that those groups will look very different from what they do now.

BE THAT DIFFERENCE. Get ahead in the game. Be you. Be the one they need in the next year, five years, twenty, and beyond. Mono flavors will be out. Multi flavors in.

All you need is a platform and a process:

Explore Find the personal and professional spaces you want to occupy. This involves trial and error.

Energize Generate the support, energy, inspiration, and drive to overcome opposition and prejudice. You're going to get pumped up!

Engage Opportunities always come. Prepare for them and leverage your toolkit when they arrive. There is no room for sitting on the sidelines.

Expand. Get in the game and test your limits. At this point you are shamelessly influencing.

* * *

There's actually a way to bake ice cream in an oven without causing it to melt, and it's edible. How wild is that? The popular name for this dish is called Baked Alaska, famously coined by Charles Ronhofer, the chef of Delmonico's in New York in 1867. Supposedly he named it in honor of Seward's purchase of Alaska from the Russians.[122]

Baked Alaska is composed of a sponge cake with ice cream on top, covered in a layer of meringue and then either baked at high heat or crusted with a blow torch. The physics of this composition are riveting. The foam portions (cake and meringue) have air pockets that keep the heat from reaching the ice cream. The finished product is a crispy meringue outside and cold ice cream cake center.

---

122 (Silver, 2016)

Our identities can be like that ice cream inside the Baked Alaska—so delicate and seemingly ill-prepared to weather heat. Yet thoughtfully crafted cake and meringue layers can guard that precious center. It's a graceful armor that transforms the separate parts into a magical whole.

All together it's delicious.

You are delicious.

REFERENCES

———

INTRODUCTION

Alesci, Cristina. "Xerox's Ursula Burns: Business Is Made for Men." CNNMoney. 2017. Accessed June 15, 2019. https://money.cnn.com/2017/02/03/technology/american-dream-ursula-burns/index.html.

Burns, Ursula. "Ursula M. Burns Shares Her Lean In Story." Lean In. 2019. Accessed June 15, 2019. https://leanin.org/stories/ursula-burns.

Elk, Kathleen. "How Calling out a VP Helped an Entry-level Employee Become CEO of Xerox." CNBC. February 07, 2017. Accessed June 15, 2019. https://www.cnbc.

com/2017/02/07/calling-out-a-vp-helped-an-entry-level-employee-become-ceo-of-xerox.html.

McCormick, Kate. "The Evolution of Workplace Diversity." THL March April 2007. 2007. Accessed June 15, 2019. http://www.thehoustonlawyer.com/aa_mar07/page10. htm.

CHAPTER 1

Berger, Guy. "Data Reveals The Most In-Demand Soft Skills Among Candidates." LinkedIn Talent Blog. August 30, 2016. Accessed June 15, 2019. https://business.linkedin. com/talent-solutions/blog/trends-and-research/2016/ most-indemand-soft-skills.

Deming, David J. "The Growing Importance of Social Skills in the Labor Market." NBER. August 14, 2015. Accessed June 15, 2019. https://www.nber.org/papers/w21473.

"The Soft Skills Stats You Need to Know." Coursera Blog. August 23, 2017. Accessed June 15, 2019. https://blog.coursera.org/soft-skills-stats-need-know/.

Ventures, Juma. "Juma." Juma Ventures. 2018. Accessed June 15, 2019. https://www.juma.org/.

CHAPTER 2

"About Blavity." Blavity. Accessed September 20, 2018. https://corporate.blavity.com/about.

Bersin, Josh. "Future of Work: The People Imperative." YouTube. November 28, 2016. Accessed June 15, 2019. https://www.youtube.com/watch?v=z8dFIc2K6eo.

"Coworking VR Space." The Armada. Accessed June 15, 2019. http://coworking.thearmada.co/.

Fuller, Joseph B., Judith K. Wallenstein, Manjari Raman, and Alice De Chalendar. "Your Workforce Is More Adaptable Than You Think." Harvard Business Review. April 16, 2019. Accessed June 15, 2019. https://hbr.org/2019/05/your-workforce-is-more-adaptable-than-you-think.

Mitchell, Julian. "Meet Morgan DeBaun: The Blavity Founder Bridging The Gap Between Content And Tech." Forbes. April 02, 2016. Accessed June 15, 2019. https://www.forbes.com/sites/julianmitchell/2015/11/05/meet-morgan-debaun-the-blavity-founder-bridging-the-gap-between-content-and-tech/#710ed185751a.

Stahler, Kelsea. "How 'Blavity' Co-Founder Morgan DeBaun Became One Of The Most Important Women In Silicon Valley." Bustle. June 12, 2019. Accessed June 15, 2019.

https://www.bustle.com/p/how-blavity-co-founder-mor-gan-debaun-became-one-of-the-most-important-wom-en-in-silicon-valley-10133055.

Tunkel, Anna. "Three Trends On The Future Of Work." Forbes. August 13, 2018. Accessed June 15, 2019. https://www.forbes.com/sites/forbesbusinessdevelopmentcoun-cil/2018/08/13/three-trends-on-the-future-of-work/.

CHAPTER 3

Blodgett, Sequoia. "Arlan Hamilton: From Tour Manager to Venture Capitalist." Black Enterprise. September 29, 2017. Accessed June 15, 2019. https://www.blackenterprise.com/arlan-hamilton-tour-manager-venture-capitalist/.

Capital, Backstage. "Front Page." Backstage Capital. Accessed September 18, 2018. https://backstagecapital.com/.

CNBC. How Arlan Hamilton Founded VC Firm Backstage Capital While Homeless. November 19, 2018. Accessed June 15, 2019. https://www.msn.com/en-us/money/mar-kets/how-arlan-hamilton-founded-vc-firm-backstage-capital-while-homeless/ar-BBPToFY.

Duckworth, Angela Lee. "Grit: The Power of Passion and Perseverance." TED. April 2013. Accessed June 15, 2019.

https://www.ted.com/talks/angela_lee_duckworth_grit_
the_power_of_passion_and_perseverance?language=en.

Hamilton, Arlan. "Dear White Venture Capitalists: If You're
Reading This, It's (almost!) Too Late." Medium. June
13, 2015. Accessed June 15, 2019. https://medium.com/
female-founders/dear-white-venture-capitalists-if-you-
re-not-actively-searching-for-and-seeding-qualified-
4f382f6fd4a7.

Hazlehurst, Beatrice. "An Afternoon Off with Tess Holliday: The Fat, Fed-Up Supermodel Ready for a Revolu-
tion." PAPER. July 12, 2018. Accessed June 15, 2019. http://
www.papermag.com/an-afternoon-off-with-tess-holli-
day-2511135424.html.

Holliday, Tess. *Not So Subtle Art of Being a Fat Girl: Loving
the Skin You're In*. Weldon Owen, Incorporated, 2017.

Kaufman, Scott Barry. "Grit: Bringing Passion Back." Scientific American Blog Network. September 19, 2018.
Accessed June 15, 2019. https://blogs.scientificamerican.
com/beautiful-minds/grit-bringing-passion-back/.

Okwodu, Janelle. "Is Fashion Ready for Plus-Size Model
Tess Holliday?" Vogue. January 18, 2018. Accessed June 15,

2019. https://www.vogue.com/article/tess-holliday-model-high-fashion-message.

Peoples, Lindsay. "How Tess Holliday Is Single-handedly Changing Beauty Standards." The Cut. November 22, 2016. Accessed June 15, 2019. https://www.thecut.com/2016/11/how-tess-holliday-is-changing-beauty-standards.html.

Rodriguez, Salvador. "How This Woman Went From Homelessness to Running a Multimillion-Dollar Venture Fund." Inc.com. August 12, 2016. Accessed June 15, 2019. https://www.inc.com/salvador-rodriguez/arlan-hamilton-backstage-capital.html.

Scott, Caitlin. "Size 22 Supermodel Tess Holliday Scores Her First Magazine Cover." Cosmopolitan. March 16, 2018. Accessed June 15, 2019. https://www.cosmopolitan.com/entertainment/news/a40789/size-22-supermodel-tess-holliday-covers-people/.

Stiffler, Lisa. "How Arlan Hamilton Turned Her Hustle and Grit into a Minority-focused VC Fund Investing Millions." GeekWire. August 02, 2018. Accessed June 15, 2019. https://www.geekwire.com/2018/arlan-hamilton-turned-hustle-grit-minority-focused-vc-fund-investing-millions/.

Tempesta, Erica. "Tess Holliday Fired Someone for Saying She Couldn't Model High Fashion." Daily Mail Online. October 06, 2018. Accessed June 15, 2019. https://www.dailymail.co.uk/femail/article-6240537/Tess-Holliday-reveals-fired-team-saying-model-high-fashion.html.

Torres, Jessica. "TESS HOLLIDAY INTERVIEW | Marriage, Mistakes, Dealing with Negativity." YouTube. April 09, 2018. Accessed June 15, 2019. https://www.youtube.com/watch?v=CoyQTCP9XDQ.

CHAPTER 4

Burns, Hilary. "Morgan Stanley's Carla Harris on Why You Need to Understand the Adjectives of Success." Bizjournals.com. October 1, 2014. Accessed June 16, 2019. https://www.bizjournals.com/bizwomen/news/profiles-strategies/2014/10/morgan-stanleys-carla-harris-on-why-you-need-to.html?page=all.

Gafni, Noa. "Three Ways Young People Are Changing the World." World Economic Forum. September 12, 2014. Accessed June 16, 2019. https://www.weforum.org/agenda/2014/09/three-ways-young-people-changing-world/.

Harris, Ainsley. "Memo to the Silicon Valley Boys' Club: Arlan Hamilton Has No Time for Your BS." Fast Company. September 21, 2018. Accessed June 16, 2019. https://www.fastcompany.com/90227793/backstage-capitals-arlan-hamilton-brings-diversity-to-venture-capital.

Harris, Carla. "2018 Catalyst Awards Conference: Carla Harris." YouTube. April 27, 2018. Accessed June 15, 2019. https://www.youtube.com/watch?v=7VWt8385Y-Y.

Harris, Carla. "Carla's Pearls." Carla Harris. 2019. Accessed June 16, 2019. https://carlaspearls.com/.

Institute, The Aspen. "Jessica O. Matthews | Founder & CEO, Uncharted Play." YouTube. March 14, 2016. Accessed September 15, 2018. https://www.youtube.com/watch?v=HaT-5JHBPHPg.

Klich, Tanya. "Uncharted Power Founder Jessica O. Matthews On Building The Anti-Silicon Valley Energy Startup." Forbes. November 20, 2018. Accessed June 16, 2019. https://www.forbes.com/sites/tanyaklich/2018/11/12/uncharted-power-founder-jessica-o-matthews-on-building-the-anti-silicon-valley-energy-startup/.

Leibowitz, Glenn. "How to Use 'Negative Motivation' to Accomplish Your Goals." Inc.com. August 27, 2018.

Accessed June 15, 2019. https://www.inc.com/glenn-lei-bowitz/how-to-use-negative-motivation-to-accomplish-your-goals.html.

Marcus, Bonnie. "Carla Harris Was Raised To Be A Winner." Forbes. March 16, 2016. Accessed June 15, 2019. https://www.forbes.com/sites/bonniemarcus/2016/03/16/carla-harris-was-raised-to-be-a-winner/#73cbde6157f4.

Power, Uncharted. "UNCHARTED POWER | Power, Redefined." About Us- Jessica Matthews. 2018. Accessed September 15, 2018. https://www.u-pwr.co/.

Safer, Morley. "The Secret to Career Success? Enthusiasm." CBS News. July 27, 2014. Accessed June 15, 2019. https://www.cbsnews.com/news/the-secret-to-career-success-en-thusiasm/.

"The Secret Advantages of Being Young." World Bank Blogs. January 2016. Accessed June 16, 2019. https://blogs.world-bank.org/governance/it-s-time-youth-and-governments-fall-love.

Zarya, Valentina. "How Morgan Stanley's Carla Harris Found Success, in Both Banking and Music." Fortune.com. March 1, 2016. Accessed June 15, 2019. http://fortune.com/2016/03/01/carla-harris-morgan-stanley/.

CHAPTER 5

Judge, Timothy A., and Robert D. Bretz, Jr. "Political Influence Behavior and Career Success." Science Direct. November 10, 2005. Accessed June 16, 2019. https://www. sciencedirect.com/science/article/pii/S0149206305800042.

Pfeffer, Jeffrey. "Jeffrey Pfeffer: How to "Lean In" to Power." Stanford Graduate School of Business. September 29, 2015. Accessed June 16, 2019. https://www.gsb.stanford. edu/insights/jeffrey-pfeffer-how-lean-power.

CHAPTER 6

Bishop, Todd. "IBM Sues Microsoft's New Chief Diversity Officer over Non-compete Agreement." GeekWire. February 16, 2018. Accessed June 16, 2019. https://www.geekwire. com/2018/ibm-sues-microsofts-new-chief-diversity-offi-cer-non-compete-agreement/.

Fairygodboss Radio: Cindy Robbins - President and Chief People Officer, Salesforce. Directed by Cindy Robbins. Performed by Cindy Robbins. Fairygodboss. 2018. Accessed June 16, 2019. https://fairygodboss.com/community-pod-cast/B1NJZN58X/fairygodboss-radio-cindy-robbins-pres-ident.

Hemmings, Jilea. "When Employees See That You Are Invested In Who They Are As People, They Are More Invested In The…" Medium. July 12, 2018. Accessed June 16, 2019. https://medium.com/authority-magazine/when-employees-see-that-you-are-invested-in-who-they-are-as-people-they-are-more-invested-in-the-1b303c6d6667.

Ries, Tonia, David M. Bersoff, Cody Armstrong, Sarah Adkins, and Jamis Bruening. "2018 Edelman Trust Barometer." 2018 Edelman Trust Barometer. 2018. Accessed June 15, 2019. https://www.edelman.com/sites/g/files/aatuss191/files/2018-10/2018_Edelman_Trust_Barometer_Global_Report_FEB.pdf.

Staff. "IBM Suit Against Former Diversity Chief Illustrates Growing Value of D&I." Talent Daily. February 14, 2018. Accessed June 16, 2019. https://www.cebglobal.com/talent-daily/ibm-suit-against-former-diversity-chief-illustrates-growing-value-of-di/.

Stahl, Lesley. "Leading by Example to Close the Gender Pay Gap." CBS News. April 15, 2018. Accessed June 16, 2019. https://www.cbsnews.com/news/salesforce-ceo-marc-benioff-leading-by-example-to-close-the-gender-pay-gap/.

CHAPTER 7

Berdahl, Jennifer L., Marianne Cooper, Peter Glick, Robert W. Livingston, and Joan C. Williams. "Work as a Masculinity Contest." *Journal of Social Issues* 74, no. 3 (September 13, 2018): 422-48. doi:10.1111/josi.12289.

Hempel, Jessi. "The Pao Effect Is What Happens After Lean In | Backchannel." Wired. November 20, 2018. Accessed June 16, 2019. https://www.wired.com/story/the-pao-effect-is-what-happens-after-lean-in/.

Pao, Ellen. "This Is How Sexism Works in Silicon Valley." Cut, 2017. https://www.thecut.com/2017/08/ellen-pao-silicon-valley-sexism-reset-excerpt.html.

CHAPTER 8

Brooks, Chad. "CEO Risk-Taking: Upbringing Could Hold the Answer." Business News Daily. January 22, 2016. Accessed June 16, 2019. https://www.businessnewsdaily.com/8733-risk-taking-social-class.html.

Hannon, Kerry. "Black Women Entrepreneurs: The Good And Not-So-Good News." Forbes.com. September 09, 2018. Accessed June 16, 2019. https://www.forbes.com/sites/nextavenue/2018/09/09/black-women-entrepreneurs-the-good-and-not-so-good-news/#3acde1816ffe.

McRoberts, Sam. "Here's What Science Says You Should Do to Achieve Greater Success." Entrepreneur. December 29, 2017. Accessed June 16, 2019. https://www.entrepreneur.com/article/305985.

Merritt, Jennifer. "Don't Call Candice Matthews (Or Her Accelerator) a Unicorn." Cincinnati Refined. August 29, 2018. Accessed June 16, 2019. http://cincinnatirefined.com/lifestyle/candice-matthews-hillman-accelerator-tech-startup-cincinnati.

Morin, Amy. "What Successful People Know About Taking Calculated Risks." Inc.com. February 27, 2017. Accessed June 16, 2019. https://www.inc.com/amy-morin/this-is-the-biggest-mistake-people-make-when-it-comes-to-taking-risks.html.

CHAPTER 9

Buettner, Dan. "How to Live to Be 100+." TED.com. September 2009. Accessed June 16, 2019. https://www.ted.com/talks/dan_buettner_how_to_live_to_be_100?language=en.

Mogi, Ken. "This Japanese Secret to a Longer and Happier Life Is Gaining Attention from Millions around the World." CNBC Make It. May 28, 2019. Accessed June 16,

2019. https://www.cnbc.com/2019/05/22/the-japanese-se-cret-to-a-longer-and-happier-life-is-gaining-attention-from-millions.html.

PARTING THOUGHTS

Silver, Maya. "Baked Alaska: A Creation Story Shrouded In Mystery." The Salt. NPR, March 29, 2016. https://www.npr.org/sections/thesalt/2016/03/29/469957638/baked-alaska-a-creation-story-shrouded-in-mystery.